BARRON'S

Traveler's Language Guides: Spanish

by
Josep Ràfols

All inquiries should be addressed to:
Barron's Educational Series, Inc.
250 Wireless Boulevard
Hauppauge, NY 11788
http://www.barronseduc.com

ISBN-13: 978-0-7641-3210-0
ISBN-10: 0-7641-3210-5
Library of Congress Control Number 2005921553

Photo sources
Bundesverband Selbsthilfe Körperbehinderter, Krautheim: 71;
Cycleurope, Bergisch-Gladbach: 56; Fordwerke AG: 54; H. Geissel,
Stuttgart: 15, 19, 45, 111, 135, 169; HB-Verlag, Ostfildern: 11, 29;
R. Kämpf, Esslingen: 75, 119; U. Messelhäuser, Salem: 67; Oficina
Española de Turismo, Munich: 85, 129; Wolpert Fotodesign,
Stuttgart: 37/38, 95-101, 141, 157

Cover: Getty Images/Stone (Chad Ehlers; John Lawrence); Getty
Images/Hulton Archive (Keystone)

Printed in China
9 8 7 6 5 4 3 2 1

Pronunciation

- All the vowels are open and must be pronounced clearly.
- **a, e,** and **o** in combination with **i, y,** or **u** form a diphthong: fue**go** *fire*; h**oy** *today*.

Pronunciation of letters in Spanish is more straightforward than in English. The following letters are pronounced just like English: **b, d, f, k, l, m, n, p, q, s, t, v, y, z.** The other letters appear on the table below.

Letter	Pronun-ciation	Rule	Spanish Example	English Example
a	ah	pronunciation always identical	rama, pata	mad, map
e	eh	pronunciation always identical	mete, sed	bed, bet
i	ih	pronunciation always identical	mira, imita	tip, active
o	oh	pronunciation always identical	pollo, mono	coin, destroy
u	uh	pronunciation always identical	mudo, tuna	rule, pull
c	s	before **e** and **i**	cerro, cima	center, cite
c	k	before **a, o, u,** or consonants	casa, coco, cuello, cresta, cloro	call, core, cure, crest, cleat
g	g	pronunciation as in English	gato, mago	great, magnum
g	Spanish j	before **e** and **i** has a strong English **h** pronunciation	gente (*hen*te), región (re*heeon*)	
gue, gui	geh, gih	the **u** is silent, except when marked by an umlaut (**ü**). In either case, the **g** sounds like the English **g**	guerra, guitarra	guest, guide
h	none	always silent	hijo, prohibir	whale, whimper
j	strong h	pronunciation sounds like the **ch** of the Scottish *loch* or the German *achtung* or *Bach*	jardín, naranja	hair, hot
r	rolled r	nonexistent in English	madre, muerte	
r	rr	at the beginning of words and after **l, n, s**	rama, sonrisa,	
w	w or v	the **w** is not a Spanish letter— it has been acquired from other languages and is pronounced according to the *original* sound.	watt, Wagner	watt (English **w** sound), Wagner (German **v** sound)
x	x	pronunciation as in English	máximo, excusa	maximum, excuse
x	Spanish J	in Mexico has a Spanish **j** pronunciation	México (me*heeko*)	
z	th	in Spain like the English **th**	maza (mah*tha*)	path, wrath
z	s	in Latin America like the English **s**	jerez, cazo	raise, cost

Stress and Accent

- Words stressed on the last syllable and ending in a vowel, **n** or **s** require a written accent: *café, después.*
- Words stressed on the penultimate (next to last) syllable and ending in a consonant (other than **n** and **s**) require a written accent: *fácil, huésped.*
- Words stressed on the antepenultimate (before the next to last) syllable always require a written accent: *música, médico, artístico.*
- Interrogative and exclamatory words always require a written accent: *quién, cómo, qué bonito.*
- Some one-syllable words always have a written accent, to distinguish them from others that are spelled the same way: *mí, tú, él, sí, sé, más.*
- **í** and **ú** when the dipththong is broken up and two separate syllables result: *día, púa, país.*
- Nouns ending in **o** are masculine; nouns ending in **a** are feminine. The gender of nouns is given in this book only for exceptions to this rule (*cura m* priest) and for other endings.

The Spanish Alphabet

A	a	[ah]	J	j	[hóhtah]	R	r	[éhrreh]
B	b	[beh]	K	k	[kah]	S	s	[éhseh]
C	c	[seh]	L	l	[éhleh]	T	t	[teh]
CH	ch	[cheh]	LL	ll	[éhyeh]	U	u	[oo]
D	d	[deh]	M	m	[éhmeh]	V	v	[veh]
E	e	[eh]	N	n	[ehneh]	W	w	[dóhbleh veh]
F	f	[éhfeh]	O	o	[oh]	X	x	[éhkees]
G	g	[heh]	P	p	[peh]	Y	y	[ee griéhgah]
H	h	[háhcheh]	Q	q	[koo]	Z	z	[zéhtah]
I	i	[ee]						

General Abbreviations

a. C.	antes de Cristo	before Christ
afmo.	afectísimo	Your obedient servant
Av.	Avenida	Avenue
AVE	Tren de Alta Velocidad Española	Spanish high-speed train
C.	Centígrado	Celsius
c.	calle	Street
Cía.	Compañía	Company

8

CV	caballo de vapor	horsepower
D.	Don	Mr.
Dª	Doña	Mrs.
d. C.	después de Cristo	a.D. (Anno Domini)
dcha.	derecha	Right
E.U.A.	Estados Unidos	United States
etc.	etcétera	etcetera
gral.	general	general
id.	ídem	ditto
incl.	inclusive	inclusive
izda.	izquierda	left
km/h	kilómetros por hora	kilometers per hour
N. B.	nota bene	NB (nota bene)
ONU	Organización de las Naciones Unidas	UN
OTAN	Organización del Tratado del Atlántico Norte	NATO
p., pág.	página	page
P. D.	posdata	PS
p. ej.	por ejemplo	for example
pl.	plaza	square
pral.	principal	main
pta.	peseta	Peseta
q.e.p.d.	que en paz descanse	May He Rest in Peace
R.A.C.E.	Real Automóvil Club de España	Royal Automobile Club of Spain
RENFE	Red Nacional de Ferrocarriles Españoles	Spanish National Railways
R.I.P.	requiescat in pace	RIP
S. A.	Sociedad Anónima	Public Corporation
Sal.	salida	exit
S. L.	Sociedad (de responsabilidad) limitada	Ltd.
sr., Sr.	señor	Mr.
sra., Sra.	señora	Mrs.
Sras.	señoras	Ladies
Sres.	señores	Gentlemen
srta., Srta.	señorita	Miss
TVE	Televisión Española	Spanish TV
UE	Unión Europea	EU (European Union)
V.° B.°	visto bueno	approval
Vd., Ud.	usted	You (sing.)
Vda.	viuda	widow
Vds., Uds.	ustedes	You (pl.)

adj	Adjective	adjetivo
adv	Adverb	adverbio
Am	Latin America	Latinoamérica
conj	Conjunction	conjunción
dat	Dative	dativo
f	Feminine	femenino
fam	Familiar	familiar, coloquial
fig	Figurative	sentido figurado
m	Masculine	masculino
n	Neuter	neutro
pers prn	Personal pronoun	pronombre personal
pl	Plural	plural
poss prn	Possessive pronoun	pronombre posesivo
prp	Preposition	preposición
sing	Singular	singular
v	Verb	verbo

Languages in Spain
Worldwide, more than 200 million people speak Spanish. This means that Spanish is the most widely spoken Romance language, spoken in Spain and in every country south of the U.S., except for a handful Portuguese- and English- speaking nations.
Since the Arabs lived on the Iberian Peninsula for many centuries, Spanish was highly influenced by Arabic. Spain's other official languages are Catalan, Basque, and Galician. They are spoken in the corresponding autonomous regions of Spain. Catalan (*català*) is spoken not only in Catalonia (Catalunya), including Barcelona, its capital, but also in the Balearic Islands and Valencia. Basque, a highly distinctive language, has little similarity with any of the Indo-European languages. Galician has a long literary tradition, especially in regard to poetry.

Different Countries, Different Customs

Intercultural Tips

Meeting and Greeting

In Spain and Latin America, men shake hands when greeting each other. Women kiss each other lightly on both cheeks.

Until about 1 P.M., people say **buenos días** in greeting. After the midday meal at the latest, they switch to **buenas tardes** and use this phrase until roughly 9 P.M. After that time—after the evening meal at the latest—they say **buenas noches.**

Forms of Address

Spaniards are relatively quick to use the familiar pronoun for "you." This is especially true of young people. If you want to address older people politely, use **usted.**

Don't be surprised if you're addressed as **guapa** (beautiful), **guapo** (handsome), or **reina** (queen) in stores, bars, or on the street. This is normally not a "come-on line," but is only meant in a friendly way. Forms of address vary in Latin America, so it is prudent to err on the formal side.

Breakfast

In general, Spaniards place little importance on breakfast. In the late morning, people drink **café con leche** (coffee with milk) or espresso in a **bar** or a **cafeteria,** and eat a **pasta** (pastry) or **churros** (short, fluted sticks of fried dough) with it. Remember that room prices in hotels usually do not include breakfast. There is an additional charge for breakfast. In Latin America breakfast is a more important affair. Bread, butter, cheese, cold cuts, and fried or soft-boiled eggs often accompany black coffee, coffee with milk, or tea.

In a Restaurant

Almost all Spanish restaurants offer a daily special at lunch: **plato del día** or **menú del día.** It is usually quite inexpensive and includes three courses: **primer plato** (appetizer), **Segundo plato** (main course), and **postre** (dessert). Often a choice of several dishes is offered. Bread and a beverage are included in the price. If you want only a light lunch, it is advisable to try the **cafeterías** with their **platos combinados,** two or more courses combined on one plate. The **plato del día** is also common throughout Latin America, but portions and courses vary from country to country.

Keep in mind that it is not customary to sit at tables that are already occupied, even if no other vacant seats are available. This applies especially to restaurants.

If you go to a restaurant with friends, it is customary to split the costs for the entire meal. Tipping is not required, but in restaurants it is expected. The amount of the tip is for you to decide. If you want to leave a tip, simply place it on the saucer on which **la cuenta** (the bill) was presented. Now you can leave without waiting for the waiter or waitress to come back.

Mealtimes

Lunch is eaten between 12 and 1 P.M., dinner between 9:30 and 10:30 P.M. in Spain and between 7:00 and 9:30 elsewhere. Don't even try going to a restaurant earlier than 9 P.M. in Spain—they will not be serving yet.

Going Out in the Evening and at Night

Nightlife starts quite late in Spain—often not until midnight—and can continue until morning. First you eat at a restaurant with friends, then go somewhere for a drink, and finally go to a disco. If you still haven't had enough, to top it all off you stop somewhere for a breakfast of **chocolate con churros.**

In general, Spain is a very child-friendly country. Even on festive occasions (city festivals, weddings, birthdays), children are part of the celebration until late into the night. All of the above may (or may not) apply to Latin America. Considering the geographic and economic diversity of the continent, uniformity never applies.

Opening Hours

Most stores open at 9 A.M. and close for lunch at 2 P.M. After lunch and the **siesta,** you can't shop again until 5 P.M. at the earliest. On the other hand, stores don't close until 8 P.M.

Large department stores are open all day, until 8 P.M. The opening hours are in effect on Saturday as well.

Telephone

People answer the phone by saying ¿diga? or ¿dígame?, or even with a short ¿sí? It is not customary to answer by giving your name. You will find plenty of telephone booths in Spain, and most of these phones accept either coins or **tarjetas telefónicas** (phone cards). If you want to place a phone call from the post office, don't go to **Correos,** but to **Telefónica,** the partially state-owned telephone company, which has now been privatized.

Highway Travel

In Spain, **autopistas** (expressways) are toll roads, and they are very expensive. There is no fee, however, for using **autovías** (divided highways) and **carreteras** (main roads). Latin American roads and highways tend to be more modest than those of Spain. Traffic is slower, but sightseeing opportunities are far greater with reduced speeds.

Lotteries

Spanish people are enthusiastic players of lotteries. The variety of tickets is astonishing: from local, daily mini-lotteries that offer prizes of a few hundred dollars, to gigantic, national enterprises that tempt you with fortunes. And in some countries you get to keep your entire prize, because the money you win there is tax-free. On the downside, not all lotteries are totally honest, so we advise you to buy tickets from national, well-known organizations.

The Christmas lotteries usually have the largest jackpots, and the interactive lotteries (where you guess the outcomes of soccer matches or other events) are gaining popularity.

Newspapers

In addition to the **prensa amarilla** or **prensa del corazón** (sensationalist newspapers), Spain also has a serious press establishment, of course, including **El País**—a daily newspaper of international repute. Especially popular are the **suplementos**, which are not restricted to Sunday publication—**El País** includes a supplement almost every day (*Babelia,* a literary supplement that appears on Saturday, *CiberP@ís,* a Thursday supplement on EDP, and *EPS,* a full-color Sunday magazine). Most Spaniards buy their paper in the morning at a newsstand, and do not have a subscription.

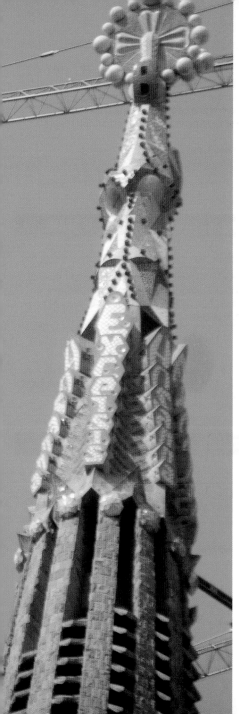

Travel Preparations

> **When you're taking a trip ...**
> Remember that a click of the mouse will provide essential
> information about your travel destination. In addition
> to information for travelers, the internet is bursting with
> information on general and specialized topics, including
> * up-to-the minute daily news for travelers, plus interesting
>   features
> * regular travel specials and contests
> * mini-guides to print and take along

Reserving a Hotel Room by E-Mail

Apreciados señores:
Quisiera reservar una habitación sencilla / doble / con dos
camas para dos noches el 24 y 25 de junio. Hagan el favor de
comunicarme si tienen habitaciones libres para esas fechas y el
precio por noche / más cena.
Atentamente,

Dear Sir or Madam,
I would like to book a single / double / twin-bedded room for
2 nights on the 24 and 25 June. Please let me know if you have
any vacancies and the total cost per night. / plus dinner.
Yours faithfully,

Renting a Car by E-Mail

Apreciads señores:
Quisiera alquilar un coche pequeño / de tamaño medio / lujoso /
de siete plazas del 20 al 25 de julio en el aeropuerto de Barajas
(Madrid) y devolverlo en Barcelona, ya que el vuelo de regreso lo
hago desde allí. Les estaría agradecido si me informaran de las
tarifas y de los documentos que es necesario presentar.
Atentamente,

Dear Sir / Madam,
I would like to hire a small / mid-range / luxury car / 7-seater
van from July 20–25 from Barajas (Madrid) I depart from
Barcelona, so I wish to leave the car there. Please inform me of
your rates and what documents I shall require.
Yours faithfully,

General Questions

I am planning to spend my vacation in… Will you please send me lodging information in that area?
Tengo la intención de pasar las vacaciones en… ¿Sería tan amable de darme información sobre dónde podría encontrar alojamiento en la zona?

What regions covered by ship cruises would you recommend?
¿Qué región es recomendable para pasar las vacaciones en un barco?

What kind of lodging do you have in mind?
¿En qué tipo de alojamiento había pensado?

>**Hotel**
>Hotel
>**Pension**
>Pensión
>**Hostel**
>Hostal
>**Apartment**
>Apartamento

Questions about Accommodations

Hotel – Pension – Bed-and-Breakfast

I am looking for an hotel, something midrange, not too expensive.
Busco un hotel, pero que no sea muy caro, de tipo medio.

I would like an hotel with an indoor swimming pool / a golf course / tennis courts.
Busco un hotel con piscina interior / campo de golf / pistas de tenis.

Could you recommend a hostel with free breakfast?
¿Me podría recomendar un hostal con desayuno incluido?

Are dogs admitted?
¿Admiten perros?

Could you put another bed in the room?
¿Se puede poner otra cama en la habitación?

How much is per week?
¿Cuánto cuesta a la semana?

Vacation Cottages/Apartments

I am looking for an apartment or a bungalow.
Busco un apartamento o un bungalow.

Where can I find a farm that offers activities for children?
¿Dónde podría encontrar una granja que tuviera actividades
para niños?

Do you have a…
¿Tiene… ?

child's bed?
una cama para niños

child's seat?
una trona

TV?
televisor

telephone?
teléfono

washer?
lavadora

dishwasher?
lavavajillas

microwave?
microondas

Is electricity included in the price?
¿Va la luz incluida en el precio?

Are bed linens and towels included?
¿Hay ropa de cama y toallas?

How much do I have to put down and when?
¿Qué paga y señal hay que hacer y cuándo?

Where and when may I pick up the key?
¿Dónde y cuándo puedo recoger la llave?

Camping

**I am looking for a campsite on the south shore. Which would
you recommend?**
Estoy buscando un cámping en la costa sur. ¿Cuál me
recomendaría?

HORA OFICIAL

General

Yes.
Sí.

No.
No.

Please.
Por favor.; *(as a reply to "Thank You!")* De nada.

Thank you!
¡Gracias!

Thanks a lot!
¡Muchas gracias!

Thanks! Same to you!
¡Gracias, igualmente!

You are welcome!
¡Por favor! / ¡No hay de qué!

Don't mention it!
¡No hay de qué!

Pardon me?
¿Cómo dice/dices?

Of course!
¡Desde luego!

All right!
¡De acuerdo!

OK!
¡De acuerdo!

Fine!
¡Está bien!

Excuse me!
¡Perdón!

Just a second, please!
¡Un momento, por favor!

That's enough!
¡Basta (ya)!

Help!
¡Ayuda!, ¡Socorro!

Who?
¿Quién?

What?
¿Qué?

Which?
¿Cuál?

To whom?
¿A quién?

How?
¿Cómo?

Where?
¿Dónde?

Where is? / Where are?
¿Dónde está?/¿Dónde están...?

Why?
¿Por qué?

What for?
¿Para qué?

How much?
¿Cuánto?

How long?
¿Cuánto tiempo?

When? / At what time?
¿Cuándo? / ¿A qué hora?

I would like...
Quisiera..., Me gustaría...

Is there...? / Are there?
¿Hay...?

Numbers—Measures—Weights

0	cero
1	un, uno
2	dos
3	tres
4	cuatro
5	cinco
6	seis
7	siete
8	ocho
9	nueve
10	diez
11	once
12	doce
13	trece
14	catorce
15	quince
16	dieciséis

17	diecisiete
18	dieciocho
19	diecinueve
20	veinte
21	veintiuno, -a, veintiún
22	veintidós
23	veintitrés
24	veinticuatro
25	veinticinco
26	veintiséis
27	veintisiete
28	veintiocho
29	veintinueve
30	treinta
31	treinta y uno, -a, treinta y un
32	treinta y dos
40	cuarenta
50	cincuenta
60	sesenta
70	setenta
80	ochenta
90	noventa
100	cien, ciento
101	ciento uno, -a
200	doscientos, -as
300	trescientos, -as
1000	mil
2000	dos mil
3000	tres mil
10,000	diez mil
100,000	cien mil
1,000,000	un millón
first	primero, primer
second	segundo
third	tercero, tercer
fourth	cuarto
fifth	quinto
sixth	sexto
seventh	séptimo
eighth	octavo
ninth	noveno
tenth	décimo
one half	medio
one third	un tercio
one fourth	un cuarto
three fourths	tres cuartos
3.5%	tres y medio por ciento

27°C	veintisiete grados Celsius
–5°C	cinco grados Celsius bajo cero
1999	mil novecientos noventa y nueve
2003	dos mil tres
millimeter	milímetro
centimeter	centímetro
meter	metro
kilometer	kilómetro
nautical mile	milla marina
square meter	metro cuadrado
square kilometer	kilómetro cuadrado
liter	litro
gram	gramo
kilogram	kilo, kilogramo

Telling the Time

Time

What time is it?
¿Qué hora es?

It is (exactly/about)...
Son (exactamente/aproximadamente)...

3 o'clock
las tres.
3:5
las tres y cinco.
3:10
las tres y diez.
3:15
las tres y cuarto.
3:30
las tres y media.
3:45
las cuatro menos cuarto.
3:55
las cuatro menos cinco.

It's 12 noon. / It's midnight.
Son las doce del mediodía/Es medianoche.

At what time? / When?
¿A qué hora? / ¿Cuándo?

At 1 o'clock
A la una.

At 2 o'clock
A las dos.

At about 4 o'clock
Alrededor de las cuatro.

In one hour
Dentro de una hora.

In 2 hours
Dentro de dos horas.

Not before 9 A.M.
No antes de las nueve de la mañana.

After 8 P.M.
Después de las ocho de la tarde.

Between 3 and 4
Entre las tres y las cuatro.

How long?
¿Cuánto tiempo?

For two hours
Durante dos horas.

From 10 to 11
Desde las diez hasta las once.

Until 5 o'clock
Hasta las cinco.

Since when?
¿Desde cuándo?

Since 8 A.M.
Desde las ocho de la mañana.

For half an hour
Por media hora.

For eight days
Por ocho días.

about noon	hacia mediodía
about this time	a esta hora
at night	por la noche
at noon	a mediodía
daily / every day	a diario, todos los días
during the day	durante el día
every day	todos los días, cada día
every hour	cada hora
in 15 days/two weeks	dentro de quince días / dos semanas

in a week	en una semana
in the afternoon/evening	por la tarde
in the morning	por la mañana
last Monday	el lunes pasado
next year	el año que viene
now	ahora
on Sunday	el domingo
on the weekend	el fin de semana
once in awhile	de vez en cuando
recently	hace poco (*Am* recién)
sometimes	a veces, algunas veces
soon	pronto
ten minutes ago	hace diez minutos
the day after tomorrow	pasado mañana
the day before yesterday	anteayer
this afternoon/evening	esta tarde
this morning	esta mañana
this week	esta semana
today	hoy
tomorrow	mañana
tomorrow afternoon/evening	mañana por la tarde
tomorrow morning	mañana por la mañana
yesterday	ayer

The Days of the Week

Monday	el lunes
Tuesday	el martes
Wednesday	el miércoles
Thursday	el jueves
Friday	el viernes
Saturday	el sábado
Sunday	el domingo

The Months

January	enero
February	febrero
March	marzo
April	abril
May	mayo
June	junio
July	julio
August	agosto
September	septiembre
October	octubre
November	noviembre
December	diciembre

The Seasons

spring	primavera
summer	verano
fall	otoño
winter	invierno

Holidays

All Saint's Day (November 1)	Todos los Santos
All Soul's Day (November 2)	el Día de los Difuntos
Ascension Day	la Ascensión
Ash Wednesday	el miércoles de ceniza
Assumption (August 15)	la Asunción
Carnival	el Carnaval
Christmas	Navidad
Christmas Eve	Nochebuena
Constitution Day (December 6)	el Día de la Constitución
Corpus Christi	el Corpus (Christi)
Easter	Pascua (de Resurrección)
Easter Monday	el Lunes de Pascua
Epiphany	los Reyes Magos, la Epifanía
Good Friday	el Viernes Santo
Hispanic Day	el Día de la Hispanidad
Holy Thursday	el Jueves Santo
Immaculate Virgin Day (December 8)	la Inmaculada (*Am* el día de la Virgen)
Labor Day (May 1)	el Día del trabajo
New Year's Day	Año Nuevo
New Year's Eve	Nochevieja
Pentecost	Pentecostés
Saint John (June 24)	San Juan
Saint Joseph (March 19)	San José

The Date

What is the date today?

¿Qué día/fecha es hoy? /¿A cuántos estamos?

Today is August 4.

Hoy es el 4 de agosto.

What fantastic/terrible weather!
¡Hace un tiempo espléndido/horroroso!

It's really cold/hot/humid.
Hace mucho frío/calor/bochorno.

It's foggy. / It's windy.
Hay niebla. / Hace (*Am* Corre) viento.

It's going to stay nice/bad.
Seguirá el buen/mal tiempo.

It's going to get warmer/colder.
Va a hacer más calor/frío.

It's going to rain/snow.
Va a llover/nevar.

There's ice on the roads.
Hay hielo en las carreteras.

Visibility is only 20 meters/less than 50 meters.
La visibilidad es de 20 metros/menos de 50 metros.

You need snow chains.
Es necesario el uso de cadenas.

air	el aire
calm	calma
cloud	la nube
cloudy	nublado
cold	frío
fog	niebla
frost	helada
glare ice	la superficie helada
gust of wind	ráfaga, racha
heat	el calor
heat wave	ola de calor
high tide	marea alta
hot	cálido, caluroso
hot, warm	caliente, cálido
humid	bochorno
ice	hielo
lightning	rayo
low tide	marea baja
rain	lluvia
rain shower	chubasco
rainy	lluvioso
snow	la nieve
sun	el sol

GENERAL

27

sunny	soleado
temperature	temperatura
thunder	trueno
variable	inestable
weather forecast	la predicción del tiempo
weather report	el boletín meteorológico
wet	húmedo
wind	viento
wind velocity	fuerza del viento

Colors

beige	beige, beis
black	negro
blue	azul
brown	marrón
colored	de colores, multicolor
golden	dorado
green	verde
grey	gris
light blue / light green	azul claro/verde claro
lilac	lila, malva
navy blue	azul oscuro/verde oscuro
orange	naranja
plain	de un solo color
red	rojo
rose	rosa
silver	plateado
turquoise	turquesa
violet	violeta
white	blanco
yellow	amarillo

Kiss, kiss
Men shake hands when they meet. Women receive a kiss—
usually an "air kiss"—on the cheek.

Saying Hello

Good morning!
¡Buenos días!

Good afternoon! *(from early afternoon till early night)*
¡Buenas tardes!

Good night!
¡Buenas tardes! / ¡Buenas noches!

Hi! How are things?
¡Hola! / ¿Qué tal?

What's your name, please? *(respectful)*
¿Cómo se llama usted, por favor?

What's your name? *(familiar tone)*
¿Cómo te llamas?

Spaniards and Latinos are quick to use the familiar pronoun.
This is especially true of young people.

My name is...
Me llamo...

Spaniards and Latinos always have two last names: the first is
the father's name, the second, the mother's name. Once
women marry, they usually do not take their husband's name,
but keep both maiden names.

How do you do? *(respectful)*
¿Qué tal está usted?

How are you? *(greeting a friend)*
¿Qué tal?, ¿Cómo estás?

Fine, thank you. And you? *(usted = respectful; tú = to a friend)*
Bien, gracias. ¿Y usted/tú?

The question "How are you?" (¿Cómo estás?) is a rhetorical one, and the usual reply is merely "fine" (bien) or "great" (muy bien). Only with very good friends or after repeated inquiries is it proper to speak openly about physical or emotional problems.

Introductions

May I introduce you to...
Le/Te presento...

Mrs. X.
a la señora X.

Mr. X.
al señor X.

my husband.
a mi marido.

my wife.
a mi esposa/mujer.

my son.
a mi hijo.

my daughter.
a mi hija.

my friend. *(male)* / **my friend.** *(female)*
a mi amigo. / a mi amiga.

Saying Good-bye

Good-bye!
¡Adiós! / ¡Hasta la vista!

See you soon!
¡Hasta pronto!

See you later!
¡Hasta luego!

See you tomorrow!
¡Hasta mañana!

Have a good time!
¡Que vaya bien!

Don't forget us!
¡No nos olviden!

Good night!
¡Buenas noches!

Bye!
¡Adiós!/¡Hasta luego!

Have a nice trip!
¡Buen viaje!

Requesting and Thanking

Please.
Por favor. (*In reply to "Thank you!"*) De nada.

Yes, please.
Sí, por favor.

No, thank you.
No, muchas gracias.

> Polite phrases like "Thank you" or "Please" are less frequently
> used in Spain than in this country, especially in a family setting
> and among good friends.

May I?
¿Permite?

Sorry to bother you.
Perdone la molestia.

Excuse me, may I ask you something?
Perdone, ¿le podría hacer una pregunta?

Could you help me, please?
¿Puede usted ayudarme, por favor?

Can I ask you for a favor?
¿Puedo/podría pedirle un favor?

Would you mind just...?
¿Sería tan amable de...?

Thank you./Thank you very much, you've been a great help.
Muchas/muchísimas gracias, me ha ayudado mucho.

That was very kind of you.
Ha sido muy amable de su parte.

Could you please tell me...?
¿Me puede decir...?

Could you recommend...?
¿Me puede recomendar... ?

Thank you!
¡Gracias!

Thank you, my pleasure!
¡Gracias, con mucho gusto!

Thanks, that's very kind of you.
Gracias, es muy amable de su parte.

You're welcome / Don't mention it.
De nada. / No hay de qué.

Excuse me!
¡Perdón!

Please accept my apologies.
¡Lo siento en el alma!

Bless you! *(after sneezing)*
¡Jesús!

Get well soon!
¡Que se mejore! / ¡Que te mejores!

Opinions and Feelings

Agreement and Conversational Responses

Good.
Bien.

Right.
Correcto.

Agreed / It's a deal.
¡De acuerdo!/¡Hecho!

All right.
¡Está bien!

OK!
¡De acuerdo!

That's it.
Exacto.

Oh!
¡Ah!

Oh, really!
¿Ah, sí?

Really?
¿No me digas?

How interesting!
¡Vaya, vaya!

How nice!
¡Qué bien!

I understand. / I see.
Ya entiendo.

That's the way it is.
Así son las cosas.

I agree entirely.
Totalmente de acuerdo contigo.

It's true.
Es verdad.

That's (really) good.
Me parece (muy) bien.

I'd love to!
¡Con mucho gusto!

Refusal

I don't want to.
No quiero.

I really don't feel like it.
No me apetece.

I don't have time.
No tengo tiempo.

I don't agree with that.
No estoy de acuerdo con esto.

That's out of the question!
¡Nada de eso!

Certainly not! / No way!
¡De ninguna manera!

Count me out!
¡Conmigo no contéis/cuentes!

I don't like that at all.
No me gusta nada de nada.

Preferences

I like it. / I don't like it.
(No) me gusta.

I'd rather...
Prefiero...

It would be better if...
Lo mejor sería...

I'd like to find out more about that.
Me gustaría tener más información sobre eso.

Expressing Ignorance

(That) I don't know.
No lo sé.

No idea.
Ni idea.

Indecision

Makes no difference to me.
Me da lo mismo.

I don't know yet.
No sé todavía.

Perhaps.
Quizás.

Probably.
Probablemente.

Delight—Enthusiasm

Great!
¡Magnífico!

Fantastic!
¡Fantástico!

Wonderful!
¡Estupendo!

Awesome!
¡Fenomenal!

Unbelievable!
¡Genial!

Contentment

I am totally pleased.
Estoy supercontento.

I can't complain.
No puedo quejarme.

That worked out perfectly.
Ha salido a las mil maravillas.

Boredom

How boring! / Talk about boring!
¡Vaya aburrimiento! / ¡Un aburrimiento que no veas!

...a total bore.
... es un rollo.

Astonishment—Surprise

Oh!
¡Ah!

Really?
¿De veras?

That's hard to believe!
¡Es increíble!

Incredible!
¡Increíble!

Relief

It's lucky that…
¡Vaya una suerte que… !

Thanks God!
¡Gracias a Dios!

Finally!
¡Por fin!/ ¡Finalmente!

Composure

Don't panic! / Don't get excited!
¡Sobre todo, calma/no ponerse nerviosos!

Don't worry about it.
No se preocupe.

Annoyance

That's aggravating!
¡Qué fastidio!

Damn!
¡Maldita sea!

That's enough!
¡Ya basta!

…I can't stand it.
… no lo soporto.

What gall! / How impertinent!
¡Vaya cara más dura! / ¡Vaya impertinencia!

That's can't be true!
¡Será posible!

Rebuking

What do you think you are doing?
¡Pero usted qué se ha creído!

Don't you dare come near me!
¡Ni se le ocurra acercárseme!

No way!
¡Ni pensarlo!

Oh no!
¡Vaya...!

I'm sorry.
Lo siento / Lo lamento mucho.

I feel really sorry for...
Siento mucho lo de...

What a shame!
¡Qué pena! / ¡Qué lástima!

Body Language

Come here! (from nearby)

Come here (from far away)

I don't know!/I don't care!

Boaster!/Show-off!

37

Not with me!

It was swarming with people.

Watch out!

The meal was fabulous!

You've got a lot of nerve!

Good luck!

Modesty is a virtue
If a Spanish or Latino man compliments you—saying, for example, that you're wearing something pretty—don't answer by saying "thank you." Instead, use some kind of disclaimer, such as "oh, this old thing" or "it was on sale."

How nice!
¡Qué bonito!

That's wonderful!
¡Esto es fantástico!

That's really nice of you!
¡Muy amable de su/tu parte!

I like you. / You're so nice.
La encuentro muy simpática/amable.

The meal was excellent!
¡La comida estaba estupenda!

This is one of the best meals we have ever had!
¡Pocas veces nos habían hecho una comida tan buena como la suya!

It's really gorgeous here!
¡Este es un lugar maravilloso!

You speak Spanish / English very well.
Habla muy bien el español/inglés.

That looks great!
¡No está mal!

We had a very nice time with you.
Hemos estado muy bien con ustedes.

beautiful	bonito
cozy, comfy	cómodo, agradable
delicious	bueno, rico, sabroso
excellent	excelente
fantastic	fantástico
friendly	amable
handsome	guapo
impressive	impresionante
pleasant	agradable
polite	amable
pretty	bonito

As almost everywhere else in the world, the three major topics of conversation are soccer, the family, and politics.

Personal Information

How old are you?
¿Qué edad tiene usted / tienes?

I'm thirty-nine.
Tengo treinta y nueve años.

What do you do (for a living)?
¿Qué profesión tiene usted / tienes?

I'm a/an
Soy...

I work in...
Trabajo en...

I'm retired.
Estoy jubilado/jubilada.

I'm still in school.
Todavía voy al colegio.

I'm a student.
Soy estudiante.

Place of Origin and Stay

Where are you form?
¿De dónde es usted / eres?

I'm from Chicago.
Soy de Chicago.

Have you been here long?
¿Lleva usted / Llevas ya mucho tiempo aquí?

I've been here since...
Estoy aquí desde...

How long are you staying?
¿Cuánto tiempo se queda / te quedas?

Is this your first time here?
¿Es la primera vez que está usted / estás aquí?

So what's your impression?
¿Qué le parece?

The Family

Are you married?
¿Está usted casado/casada?

Do you have any children?
¿Tiene hijos?

Yes, but they are already grown-up.
Sí, pero ya son mayores.

How old are your children?
¿Cuántos años tiene su hijo/hija?

My daughter is eight (years old) and my son is five (years old).
Mi hija tiene 8 (años) y mi hijo 5.

Hobbies

➢ also Active Vacations and Creative Vacations

Do you have any hobbies?
¿Tiene / tienes algún hobby?

I devote a lot of time to my kids.
Dedico mucho tiempo a mis hijos.

I like very much to read.
Me gusta mucho leer.

I surf a lot in the internet.
Paso mucho tiempo en Internet.

I like to work in the garden.
Me gusta trabajar en el jardín.

I paint a bit.
Pinto un poco.

I collect antiques/stamps.
Colecciono antigüedades/sellos.

What are your interests?
Y sus intereses, ¿cuáles son?

I am interested in...
Me interesa...

I participate in...
Participo en...

...is one of my favorite pastimes.
... es una de mis ocupaciones preferidas.

cook, to	cocinar
create pottery, to	hacer cerámica
do handicrafts, to	hacer bricolaje
do nothing, to	no hacer nada

draw, to	dibujar
learn languages, to	aprender idiomas
listen to music, to	escuchar música
paint, to	pintar
play an instrument, to	tocar un instrumento
practice sports, to	hacer deporte
read, to	leer
relax, to	descansar
travel, to	viajar
work in the garden, to	trabajar en el jardín

Fitness

➢ also Active Vacations

How do you keep in shape?
¿Cómo se mantiene usted en forma?

I jog./I swim./I ride a bike.
Corro. / Nado. / Voy en bicicleta.

I play tennis/volleyball once a week.
Una vez por semana juego al tenis/voleibol.

I go to the health club on a regular basis.
Voy con bastante frecuencia al gimnasio.

What kind of sport do you practice?
¿Qué deporte practica usted?

I play...
Juego a...

I am fan of...
Soy aficionado a...

I like to go to...
Me gusta ir a...

May I also play?
¿Puedo jugar yo también?

Making a Date

Do you have any plans for tomorrow evening?
¿Tiene usted / Tienes algún plan para mañana por la noche?

Would you like to go out with me?
¿Quiere usted / Quieres que vayamos juntos?

Should we go out this evening and do something?
¿Quiere usted / Quieres que hagamos algo juntos esta noche?

I would like to take you to dinner tomorrow.
Me gustaría invitarle/invitarla/invitarte mañana a cenar.

At what time should we meet?
¿A qué hora nos encontraremos?

We could meet at 9 o'clock in front of.../at
Podemos encontrarnos a las nueve delante de... / en...

I'll pick you up.
Le/La/Te recogeré.

I would like to see you again.
Me agradaría volver a verle/verla/verte.

Thank you for a very nice time!
¡Ha sido una velada estupenda!

Flirting

> Don't be surprised if you're addressed as *guapo* (handsome) or *reina* (queen) in stores, bars, or on the street. Normally this is not a "come-on line," but a common form of address in Spain, meant in a friendly way.

You have beautiful eyes.
Tienes unos ojos preciosos.

I like the way you smile.
Me gusta como sonríes.

I like you.
Me gustas.

I love to be with you.
Me encanta estar contigo.

I think you are great!
¡Te encuentro fantástico/fantástica!

I love you.
Te quiero.

Do you have a steady boyfriend/girlfriend?
¿Tienes novio/novia?

Do you live with somebody?
¿Vives con alguien?

Are you married?
¿Estás casado/casada?

I am separated. / We do not live together.
Estoy separado/separada. / No vivimos juntos.

Do you want to come to my place?
¿Vamos a mi casa?

No, slow down a moment.
No, me parece demasiado precipitado.

We could have a few kisses.
Podemos darnos unos besos.

Please leave!
Ahora vete, por favor.

Please leave me alone!
¡Por favor, déjeme en paz!

Stop that immediately!
¡Haga el favor de parar de una vez!

Communication Problems

Pardon me?
¿Cómo dice/dices?

I can't understand you.
No le/la entiendo.

Could you please repeat that?
¿Puede repetir, por favor?

Could you please speak a bit slower?
Por favor, hable un poco más despacio.

I understand.
Entiendo.

Do you speak...
¿Habla usted / Hablas...

> **German?**
> alemán?
> **Spanish?**
> español?
> **English?**
> inglés?
> **French?**
> francés?

I only speak a bit of...
Hablo sólo un poco de...

Could you please write down for me?
¿Me lo podría escribir, por favor?.

Horn concerts

In Spain's bigger cities, the traffic is heavy, but not chaotic. People drive fast, but they look out for other drivers and motorcyclists. Often you will hear horns honking: This doesn't necessarily mean that someone is a bad driver or needs to watch out, but perhaps that the driver wants to greet a friend or that his favorite soccer team has just won a game.

In the large cities, you'll quickly learn that in Spain and Latin America they adore motorcycles: the streets are full of them. Bicycles, by the way, are not considered means of transportation in Spain; they are used only for recreation.

Be careful! In summer, you'll have to expect long lines of traffic on all roads leading to beaches—particularly on the weekend, of course.

Asking for Directions

Useful Words

across from	frente a, enfrente de
after	después de
behind	detrás de
curve	curva
far	lejos
here	aquí
in front of	delante de
intersection	el cruce
left	a la izquierda
near	cerca
next to	junto a
right	a la derecha
straight ahead	todo seguido/derecho
street	la calle
street corner	la esquina
there	allí
traffic light	semáforo, disco

Directions

Excuse me, how do I get to...?
Perdón, ¿cómo se va a...?

Go straight ahead until...
Todo seguido (*Am* derecho) hasta...

46

Then turn left/right at the traffic light.
Luego en el semáforo tuerza (*Am* doble) a la izquierda/derecha.

Follow the signs.
Siga los letreros.

Is it far from here?
¿Queda muy lejos de aquí?

It's really close from here.
Está muy cerca de aquí.

Excuse me, Madam/Miss/Sir, is this the road to...?
Perdón, señora/señorita/señor, ¿es ésta la carretera de...?

Excuse me, Madam/Miss/Sir, where is ... please?
Perdón, señora/señorita/señor, ¿dónde está...?

I am sorry, but I don't know.
Lo siento, pero no lo sé.

I am not from here.
No soy de aquí.

Go straight ahead. / Turn left/turn right.
Todo seguido (*Am* derecho). / Tuerza (*Am* Doble) a la izquierda/derecha.

The first/second street on the left/right.
La primera/segunda calle a la izquierda/a la derecha.

Cross...
Atraviese...

  the bridge.
  el puente.

  the square.
  la plaza.

  the street.
  la calle.

Best would be to take bus number...
Lo mejor es que tome el autobús número...

At the Border

Passport Check

Your passport, please.
Su pasaporte, por favor.

Do you have a visa?
¿Tiene usted un visado (*Am* una visa)?

Can I get a visa here?
¿Puedo conseguir un visado (*Am* una visa) aquí mismo?

Spain is part of the European Union, which should make travel
to and from any other European country an easy undertaking,
although it is still a good idea to carry your passport at all
times.

Customs

Do you have anything to declare?
¿Tiene usted algo que declarar?

Please pull over to the right/left.
Aparque aquí a la derecha/a la izquierda, por favor.

Please open the trunk/this suitcase.
¿Quiere abrir el portaequipajes (*Am* baúl) / esta maleta (*Am* valija), por favor?

Do I have to pay duty on this?
¿Hay que pagar derechos de aduana por esto?

Personal Data

Date of birth	fecha de nacimiento
divorced	divorciado/divorciada
married	casado/casada
single	soltero/soltera
widow/widower	viudo/viuda
First name	el nombre (de pila)
Last name	apellido
Maiden name	el nombre de soltera
Marital status	estado civil
Nationality	la nacionalidad
Place of birth	el lugar de nacimiento
Place of residence	domicilio

Border

Arrival	entrada
Border	frontera
Customs	aduana
Customs duty	los derechos de aduana
Departure	salida, partida
Driver's license	permiso/el carnet de conducir
Duty-free	exento de derechos de aduana
ID	el carnet/documento de identidad (*Am* cédula personal)
International vaccination certificate	certificado internacional de vacunación
License plate	(placa de) matrícula

Nationality sticker	placa de nacionalidad
Passport	el pasaporte
Passport control	el control de pasaporte
Residence card	tarjeta de residencia
Subject to duty	sujeto a derechos de aduana
U.S. citizen	ciudadano de E.U.A.
Valid	válido
Visa	visado (*Am* visa)

Cars and Motorcycles

Expressways (*autopistas*) are toll roads and very expensive in Spain. There is no charge for using divided highways (*autovías*) and main roads (*carreteras*).

Roadways, Regulations ...

Fine	multa
Highway	autopista
Hitchhike, to	hacer autostop
Hitchhiker	el/la autostopista
Lane	pista
Legal alcohol limit	el índice de alcoholemia
Main street	la calle principal
Radar speed check	el control de radar
Rest area	área de reposo
Road	carretera
Road sign	el indicador de camino
Service area	área de servicio
Side street	la calle lateral
Toll	el peaje
Traffic jam	atasco, embotellamiento

Hitchhike only in an emergency
Hitchhiking is not viewed with favor in Spain. You should resort to hitchhiking only under unusual circumstances (completely broke, missed your train ...). Ride-sharing centers, too, are largely unknown there.
Hitchhiking in Latin America can be dangerous. Do not attempt it alone.

Signs and Information

Conduzca lentamente	Drive slowly
Aduana	Customs
Alta tensión	High voltage
Estrechamiento	Road narrows
Atención	Caution
Bajada peligrosa	Steep hill
Callejón sin salida	Dead end
Cambio de pista	Change lanes
Camino en mal estado	Unsafe road
Cerrado al tráfico	Closed to traffic
Circulación doble	Two-way road
Circunvalación	Bypass
Conducir por la derecha	Stay on the right
Congestión del tráfico	Traffic jam
Cruce	Crossing
Curva peligrosa	Dangerous curve
Choque	Accident
Dejar libre la salida	Keep clear
Cruce de tren	RR crossing
Desviación	Detour
Dirección única	One way
Resbaladizo cuando llueve	Slippery when wet
Disminuir la marcha	Reduce speed
Embotellamiento	Bottleneck
Escuela	School
Estacionamiento	Parking
Policía de autopista	State troopers
Parquímetro	Parking meter
Luces de estacionamiento	Parking lights
Hospital	Hospital
Limitación de peso	Weight limit
Límite de velocidad	Speed limit
Niños	Children
Obras	Road work ahead
Boca de incendio	Fire hydrant
Paso de peatones / de cebra	Pedestrian crossing
Paso subterráneo	Pedestrian underpass
Peligro	Danger
Pista de bicicletas	Bike path
Precaución	Caution
Principiante	Student driver
Prohibido adelantar	No passing
Prohibido aparcar	No parking
Prohibido detenerse	No stopping
No virar en U	No U-turn
Prohibido girar a la derecha	No right turn

Prohibida la entrada	Do not enter
Prohibido virar	No turns
Puente	Bridge
Respetar la precedencia	Yield right of way
Salida	Exit
Salida de la autopista	Ramp
Semáforo	Traffic light
Tomar la fila de la izquierda	Keep left
Tomar la fila de la derecha	Keep right
Despacio	Slow
Túnel	Tunnel
Peaje	Toll
Puente de peaje	Toll bridge
Zona de peatones	Pedestrian zone

At the Gas Station

➢ also At the Garage

Where is the nearest gas station, please?
¿Dónde está la estación de servicio más cercana, por favor?

I would like ... liters of ...
Quisiera por favor... litros de...

  regular gas.
  gasolina normal.

  premium.
  súper.

  diesel.
  diesel.

  mixed.
  mezcla.

  lead-free / ... octane.
  sin plomo. / de... octanos.

Thirty euros worth of premium, please.
Súper, por favor; 30 euros.

Fill her up, please.
Lleno, por favor.

Will you please check ...
¿Quiere comprobar...

  the oil?
  el nivel del aceite?

  the air pressure?
  la presión de las ruedas?

I would like a road map of this area, please.
Quisiera un mapa de carreteras de esta zona, por favor.

Parking

Excuse me, where can I park around here?
Perdón, ¿hay algún sitio para aparcar por aquí cerca?

May I leave the car here?
¿Puedo dejar el coche aquí?

Is this parking place under surveillance?
¿Es un estacionamiento vigilado?

How much is it per hour?
¿Cuál es el precio del aparcamiento por hora?

Is this parking place open all night?
¿Está el aparcamiento abierto toda la noche?

A Breakdown

My car has broken down.
Tengo una avería.

Is there a garage nearby?
¿Hay algún taller por aquí cerca?

Could you call the emergency road service, please?
¿Puede usted por favor llamar al servicio de asistencia técnica en carretera?

Could you send me a mechanic / a tow truck?
¿Puede usted enviarme un mecánico / un coche-grúa?

Could you lend me some gas, please?
¿Podría usted darme un poco de gasolina, por favor?

Could you help me change the tire, please?
¿Podría usted ayudarme a cambiar la rueda?

Could you please give me a ride to the nearest auto repair shop?
¿Puede usted llevarme hasta el taller más próximo?

breakdown	avería
emergency phone	el poste de socorro
emergency road service	asistencia técnica en carretera
flat tire	rueda pinchada
gas canister	el bidón (*Am* el tanque) de gasolina
intermittent horn/flasher alarm	el sistema de alarma intermitente
jack	gato, el alzacoches
jumper cable	el cable eléctrico de encendido
spare wheel	rueda de repuesto
tools	las herramientas
tow cable	el cable de remolque

tow truck	grúa, el coche-grúa
tow, to	remolcar
towing service	servicio de remolque
triangular safety reflector ..	la señal de situación de peligro

At the Garage

The engine will not start.
Mi coche no arranca.

There is something wrong with the engine.
El motor no funciona bien.

...is/are faulty.
... está/están estropeado/s.

The car loses oil.
El coche pierde aceite.

Will you please have a look?
¿Puede usted mirar, por favor?

Fix only what's absolutely necessary.
Haga sólo las reparaciones estrictamente necesarias.

When will the car/the motorcycle be ready?
¿Cuándo estará arreglado el coche / arreglada la moto?

What do you suppose it will cost?
¿Cuánto costará más o menos?

air filter	filtro de aire
alarm system	(dispositivo de) alarma
alternator	la dínamo
antifreeze	el anticongelante
automatic transmission	cambio automático
blinker	el intermitente
brake	freno
brake fluid	líquido de frenos
brake lights	las luces de frenado
brights/bright lights	la luz de carretera
bumper	el parachoques (*Am* el paragolpes)
clutch	el embrague
coolant	(el) agua del radiador
defect	avería, defecto
dimming light	la luz de cruce
electronic immobilizer	el inmovilizador antirrobo
engine	el motor
gas pedal	el pedal del gas
gas pump	bomba de gasolina
gas tank	depósito

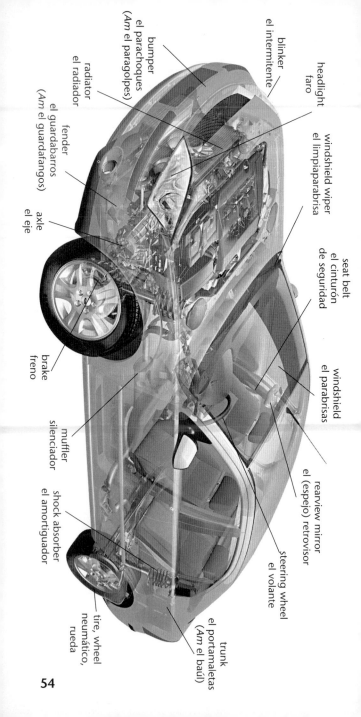

blinker
el intermitente

headlight
faro

bumper
el parachoques
(Am el paragolpes)

radiator
el radiador

fender
el guardabarros
(Am el guardafangos)

axle
el eje

windshield wiper
el limpiaparabrisas

seat belt
el cinturón
de seguridad

windshield
el parabrisas

rearview mirror
el (espejo) retrovisor

brake
freno

muffler
silenciador

shock absorber
el amortiguador

steering wheel
el volante

trunk
el portamaletas
(Am el baúl)

tire, wheel
neumático,
rueda

54

gear	marcha, la velocidad
first gear	primera (marcha)
neutral	punto muerto
reverse gear	marcha atrás
gearbox	caja de cambio
headlight	faro
hood	capó, capota
horn	bocina, el claxon
ignition	encendido (*Am* la ignición)
muffler	silenciador
oil	el aceite
oil change	cambio de aceite
parking brake	freno de mano
parking lights	la luz de posición / de estacionamiento
radiator	el radiador
rearview mirror	el (espejo) retrovisor
repair shop	el taller
screw	tornillo
seat belt	el cinturón de seguridad
short circuit	cortocircuito
spark plug	bujía
speedometer	velocímetro , cuentakilómetros
starter	el motor de arranque
taillights	las luces traseras
tire	neumático
trunk	maletero
wheel	rueda
windshield	el parabrisas
windshield wiper	el limpiaparabrisas
winter tire	neumáticos de invierno

Accident

There's been an accident.
Ha habido un accidente.

Please call right away...
Llame enseguida...

an ambulance
a una ambulancia.

the police
a la policía.

the fire department
a los bomberos.

Do you have a first-aid kit?
¿Tiene usted botiquín de urgencia?

You...
Usted...
didn't yield.
no ha respetado la preferencia.
didn't signal your turn.
no ha encendido el intermitente.

You...
Usted...
were going too fast.
iba demasiado deprisa.
ran a red light.
ha pasado con el semáforo en rojo.

Please give me your name and address.
¿Puede usted darme su nombre y dirección?

Thank you very much for your help.
Muchas gracias por su ayuda.

Car, Motorcycle, and Bike Rental

seat
el sillín

gears
cambio de marchas

handlebars
el manillar

pump
bomba de aire

front light
las luces
delanteras

back light
las luces traseras

brake
freno

tube
neumático

tire
cubierta
(de neumático)

chain
la cadena

pedal
el pedal

wheel
rueda

spoke
radio

hub
cubo
(de bicicleta)

I would like to rent... for two days/for a week...
Quisiera alquilar por dos días / una semana...
an SUV.
un coche (todo terreno).
a motorcycle.
una moto.
a bicycle.
una bicicleta.

56

How much does it cost per day/week?
¿Qué tarifa se paga por día/semana?

Does that include unlimited kilometers?
¿Está incluido el kilometraje ilimitado?

How much do you charge per kilometer?
¿Cuánto se paga por cada kilómetro de recorrido?

Is the vehicle covered by comprehensive insurance?
¿Está el vehículo asegurado a todo riesgo?

Can I surrender the vehicle in ...?
¿Es posible entregar el vehículo en...?

child's car seat	silla de niño
collision and liability insurance	seguro contra riesgos parciales
comprehensive and liability insurance	seguro a todo riesgo
deposit	fianza
deposit, to	depositar
documents	los documentos
driver's license	permiso de conducción, carnet de conducir
health insurance card	carta verde (del seguro)
helmet	casco
ignition key	la llave de encendido
kidney belt	riñonera
sun roof	techo corredizo
weekend special	tarifa de fin de semana

Airplane

Making a Flight Reservation

At what time does the next plane leave for ...?
¿A qué hora sale el próximo avión para...?

Are there still sits available?
¿Hay todavía plazas libres?

I would like to reserve a one-way flight to ...
Quisiera reservar un vuelo de ida a...

I would like to reserve a round-trip flight to ...
Quisiera reservar un vuelo de ida y vuelta a...

How much is a tourist/first class ticket?
¿Cuánto cuesta, por favor, el vuelo en clase turista / en primera clase?

I would like to sit...
Quisiera estar por favor...

   the window.
   al lado de la ventanilla.

   by the aisle.
   al lado del pasillo.

I would like to cancel this flight.
Quisiera anular este vuelo.

I would like to change this flight.
Quisiera cambiar el vuelo.

At the Airport

Where is the ... counter?
¿Dónde está, por favor, la facturación / el mostrador de la compañía...?

May I see your ticket?
¿Me permite ver su billete?

May I carry this as carry-on luggage?
¿Puedo llevar esto como equipaje de mano?

On Board

Could I have a glass of water, please?
¿Me puede traer un vaso de agua, por favor?

Could I have a pillow / blanket, please?
¿Me puede traer otro cojín / otra manta, por favor?

Would you mind switching places with me?
¿Le importaría cambiarme el sitio?

Arrival

➢ also Lost-and-Found Office

My luggage is missing.
Mi equipaje se ha perdido.

My suitcase has been damaged.
Mi maleta (*Am* valija) se ha estropeado.

Where does the bus to ... leave from?
¿De dónde sale el autobús hacia...?

➢ also Train

airline	compañía aérea
airport	aeropuerto
airport shuttle	el autobús del aeropuerto
airport tax	los derechos de aeropuerto

arrival	llegada
arrival time	hora de llegada
baggage cart	carro portaequipajes
baggage check-in	la facturación de equipajes
baggage claim	entrega de equipaje
boarding pass	tarjeta de embarque
cancel, to	anular
change the booking, to	cambiar el vuelo
check-in, to	facturar
connection	el empalme
delay	retraso
domestic flight	vuelo nacional
duty-free shop	tienda de venta libre de impuestos
emergency chute	el tobogán de emergencia
emergency exit	salida de emergencia
emergency landing	el aterrizaje forzoso
excess baggage	exceso de peso
flight	vuelo
flight attendant	el/la auxiliar de vuelo; la azafata (*Am* aeromoza)
gate	puerta
international flight	vuelo internacional
landing	el aterrizaje
life vest	chaleco salvavidas
luggage	el equipaje
passenger	pasajero
pilot	piloto
scheduled takeoff	salida regular
security charges	tasa de seguridad
security check	el control de seguridad
stopover	escala, transbordo
takeoff	el despegue
terminal	la terminal

Train

Buying Tickets

Two one-way tickets to ... , please.
Dos billetes para... , ida solo por favor.

business class / first class
2.ª clase/ 1.ª clase

No smoking
No fumar

One return-trip ticket for …, please.
Por favor, un billete de vuelta para…

Is there a reduction for children/students/senior citizens?
¿Hacen ustedes descuento para niños/estudiantes/jubilados?

I would like to reserve two non-smoking seats, please.
Quisiera reservar dos plazas de no fumadores:

to Madrid
para Madrid

on (day) … at (hour) …
el (día)… a la(s)…

in a berth car
en coche con litera

in a sleeping car
en coche-cama

with a restaurant car
con coche-restaurante

Is there a vehicle-carrying train/Autoexpress to …?
¿Hay un tren con transporte de vehículos/AutoExpreso para…?

At what time does the train to … depart from … ?
¿A qué hora sale en… el tren que va a…?

How often do I have to change trains?
¿Cuántos transbordos tengo que hacer?

(Where) Must I change trains?
¿(Dónde) Tengo que hacer transbordo?

At the Train Station

I would like to check this bag through.
Quisiera facturar esta maleta (*Am* valija).

Where can I check in my bicycle?
¿Dónde puedo facturar mi bicicleta?

Which track does the … train leave from?
¿De qué andén sale el tren para…?

Train number … from … will arrive about ten minutes late.
El tren número…, procedente de… llegará con unos diez minutos de retraso.

On the Train

Is this seat taken?
¿Está libre este asiento?

Do you mind if I open/shut the window?
¿Le importa si abro/cierro la ventanilla?

Excuse me, I believe you have taken my seat. I have reserved this seat.
Perdón, creo que se ha sentado en mi sitio. Esta plaza la tengo reservada.

Signs and Information

Agua no potable	Non-drinking water
Andén	Platform
Caballeros	Men (restroom)
Coche-cama (*Am* coche-dormitorio)	Sleeping car
Coche-literas	Berth car
Coche restaurante	Restaurant car
Consigna	Baggage check
Consigna automática	Automatic baggage check
Despacho de billetes (*Am* boletería)	Ticket counter
Freno de alarma	Emergency brake
Fumadores	Smoking section
Horario	Timetable
Información	Information
Jefe de estación	Stationmaster
Lavabo	Washroom
Libre	Free
Llegada	Arrival
No fumadores	Non-smoking section
Ocupado	Occupied
Paso a los andenes	Entry to tracks
Paso subterráneo	Underground walkway
Refrescos	Refreshments
Sala de espera	Waiting room
Salida	Exit
Señoras	Women (restroom)
Servicio sanitario (*Am* asistencia pública)	Medical help
Vía	Track
W.C. / Lavabos	Restrooms

➢ **also Airplane**

Aisle	pasillo
Arrival	llegada
Attendant	acompañante
Automatic baggage check	consigna automática
Baggage check-in	ventanilla de equipajes
Baggage deposit	consigna (de equipajes)

61

Cafeteria car	bar/cafetería
Car number	número del vagón
Car train	el autotrén
Compartment	departamento (*Am* compartimiento)
Conductor	conductor
Departure	salida, partida
Discount	descuento, la reducción
EC (EuroCity)	EC
Fare	precio del billete
Get off, to	bajar
Get on, to	subir
Half-fare (children's) ticket	el billete (*Am* boleto) infantil
Handicapped person	persona discapacitada
Head conductor	revisor-jefe
IC (InterCity)	IC (InterCity)
ICE (InterCityExpress)	ICE (InterCityExpress)
Luggage	el equipaje
Main station	la estación central
Minibar	minibar
Non-smoking compartment	departamento (*Am* compartimiento) de no fumadores
Reservation	reserva
Restaurant car	el coche restaurante
Round-trip ticket	el billete de ida y vuelta
Scenic car	el vagón abierto
Seat reservation	reserva de asiento
Smoking compartment	departamento (*Am* compartimiento) de fumadores
Stop	parada
Surcharge	suplemento
Ticket	el billete (*Am* boleto)
Ticket counter	ventanilla (*Am* boletería)
Ticket inspection	el control de billetes (*Am* boletos)
Ticket inspector	revisor
Timetable	horario
Track	el andén
Train	el tren
Train crew	personal del tren
Train station	la estación
Waiting room	sala de espera
Wheelchair user	persona con silla de ruedas
Window seat	asiento junto a la ventanilla

Information

Could you please tell me when the next ship/the next ferry for … leaves?
¿Podría decirme cuándo sale el próximo barco / el próximo transbordador (*Am* ferryboat) para…?

How long does the crossing take?
¿Cuánto dura la travesía?

When do we land at …?
¿Cuándo atracamos en…?

How long are we stopping at …?
¿Cuánto tiempo nos detenemos en…?

I would like…
Quisiera…

  a ticket for …
  un pasaje para…

  a first class ticket.
  un billete de primera clase

  a tourist class ticket.
  un billete de clase turista

  a single cabin.
  un camarote individual

  a double cabin.
  un camarote doble

I would like a ticket to visit …
Quisiera un pasaje para la excursión de las…

On Board

Where is the dining room/lounge, please?
¿Dónde está el comedor / el salón, por favor?

I don't feel well.
No me siento bien.

Could you please call the ship's doctor?
¿Me haría el favor de llamar al médico de bordo?

Could you please give me something for seasickness?
¿Puede usted darme un remedio para el mareo?

Booking	reserva
Cabin	cabina
Captain	el capitán
Coastline	costa

Cruise	crucero
Deck	cubierta
Excursion	la excursión
Ferry	el transbordador (*Am* el ferryboat)
car ferry	el transbordador de automóviles
Hovercraft	el aerodeslizador
Hydrofoil	el hidroala, el hidrofoil
Land at, to	atracar en, hacer escala en
Life preserver	el salvavidas
Life vest	chaleco salvavidas
Lifeboat	el bote salvavidas
Mainland	tierra firme
Port	puerto
Rough sea	el oleaje
Seasick, to be	estar mareado/mareada
Steamship	el vapor
Ticket	el billete (*Am* boleto)
Wharf	el muelle

Local Public Transportation

Excuse me, where is the nearest...
Por favor, ¿dónde está la próxima...

bus stop?
parada del autobús?

streetcar?
parada del tranvía?

subway stop/station?
parada/estación del metro?

Which line goes to ..., please?
¿Cuál es la línea que va a..., por favor?

When does the first/last subway leave for ...?
¿Cuándo sale el primer/último metro para...?

Excuse me, does this bus go to ...?
Perdone, ¿es éste el autobús para...?

How many stops till ...?
¿Cuántas paradas hay hasta...?

Excuse me, where do I have to get off/change?
Perdone, ¿dónde tengo que bajar/cambiar?

Could you please tell me when I have to get off?
Haga el favor de avisarme cuando tenga que bajar.

A ticket to ..., please.
Un billete (*Am* boleto) a..., por favor.

The ticket machine is broken.
El expendedor de billetes está estropeado/defectuoso.

The ticket machine takes coins only.
El expendedor de billetes sólo acepta monedas.

Bus	el autobús
Bus station	la estación de autobuses
City bus	el autobús (urbano)
Cog railway	el ferrocarril de cremallera
Conductor	el conductor
Day pass	abono diario, el billete válido para un solo día
Departure	salida
Direction	la dirección
End of the line	la estación final
Fare	precio del billete
Get on, to	subir
Local train	el tren de cercanías
Long-distance bus	el coche de línea, el autobús inter-urbano
Multi-trip ticket	el billete (*Am* boleto) multiviaje
Stamp one's ticket, to	sellar
Stop	parada
Streetcar	el tranvía
Subway	metro
Ticket	el billete (*Am* boleto)
Ticket inspector	el revisor
Ticket machine	máquina expendedora de billetes (*Am* boletos)
Ticket-canceling machine	máquina canceladora de billetes (*Am* boletos)
Timetable	horario
Trolley bus	el trolebús
Weekly ticket	el billete/abono semanal

Taxi

Excuse me Sir/Madam/Miss, where is the nearest taxi stand?
Perdón, señor/señora/señorita, ¿dónde está la parada de taxis más cercana?

To the station, please.
A la estación, por favor.

To the ... Hotel, please.
Al hotel..., por favor.

To ... Street, please.
A la calle..., por favor.

To ..., please.
A..., por favor.

How much will it cost to ...?
¿Cuánto cuesta hasta...?

Could you stop here, please?
Pare aquí, por favor.

That's for you.
Para usted.

Keep the change.
Quédese con el cambio.

Buckle up, to	ponerse el cinturón
Flat rate	precio global/total
House number	número de la casa
Kilometer rate	precio por kilómetro
Receipt	recibo
Seat belt	cinturón de seguridad
Stop, to	parar
Taxi driver	el/la taxista
Taxi stand	parada de taxis
Tip	propina

Children welcome

In general, Spain and Latin America are friendly toward children. Even on festive occasions (city festivals, weddings, birthdays), children remain part of the celebrations until late into the night.

Although many places lack special facilities (baby monitor, child seat for bikes, etc.), people go to great lengths to make the stay as pleasant and comfortable for children as possible.

Useful Questions

Is there a playground around here?
¿Hay aquí un parque infantil?

Do you have a child-care service here?
¿Hay aquí alguien que se ocupe de los niños?

How old do you have to be?
¿A partir de qué edad?

Do you know someone who could take care of our children?
¿Conoce usted a alguien que pueda ocuparse de nuestros niños?

Do you have a baby monitor?
¿Tiene usted un interfono de bebés?

Are there activities for children?
¿Hay actividades para los niños?

Do you offer a reduction for children?
¿Se hacen descuentos a los niños?

Excuse me, where can I find the nearest toy store?
Perdone, ¿dónde está la tienda de juguetes más cercana?

Could you tell me where can I find diapers?
¿Sabría dónde puedo encontrar pañales?

On the Road

We are traveling with a child. Could we have seats toward the front?
Viajamos con un niño. ¿Podríamos sentarnos en una de las primeras filas?

Do you have a child's seat belt?
¿Tiene usted cinturón de seguridad para niños?

Would you have some crayons and paper/a coloring book for our son/daughter?
¿No tendría usted colores y papel / un cuaderno de colorear para nuestro hijo/nuestra hija?

Do you rent children's car seats?
¿Alquilan sillas de niños para el coche?

In a Restaurant

Could you please bring us a high chair?
¿Podría traernos una silla de niño, por favor?

Do you serve children's portions?
¿Hacen raciones para niños?

Could you warm up this baby bottle, please?
¿Me podría calentar el biberón, por favor?

Is there a room where I can change my baby's diaper?
¿Hay alguna habitación donde pueda cambiar al niño?

Where could I breast-feed my baby?
¿Dónde puedo dar el pecho al niño?

Amusement park	el parque de atracciones
Baby car seat	silla de bebé para el coche
Baby food	comida para bebés (papillas)
Baby monitor	interfono de bebés
Babysitter	la/el canguro
Bottle warmer	el calienta-biberones
Boy	niño
Cap	gorra
Changing table	el cambiador, la mesa para cambiar los pañales
Child's bicycle seat	silla de niños para la bicicleta
Child's car seat	silla de niños para el coche
Child's seat cushion	el cojín de niños para el coche
Child-care service	guardería infantil
Children's clothing	ropa para niños
Children's reduction	descuento para niños
Coloring book	cuaderno de colorear
Crib	cuna
Diapers	los pañales
Feeding bottle	el biberón
Girl	niña
Kiddy pool	piscina infantil
Nipple	el chupete

Pediatric	pediátrico
Playground	el parque de recreo infantil
Playmate	amiguito
Sandbox	el cajón de arena
Sandcastle	castillo de arena
Sunscreen	crema para el sol
Swim ring	el flotador
Swimming lessons	curso de natación
Toys	los juguetes
Water wings	los flotadores (de brazos)

Health

Could you tell me if there is a pediatrician here?
¿Sabe usted si hay un pediatra aquí?

My child has...
El niño (Mi hijo) tiene...

He/She is allergic to...
El niño (Mi hijo) es alérgico a...

He/she has thrown up.
Ha vomitado.

He/she has diarrhea.
Tiene diarrea

He/she has been stung.
El niño / la niña tiene picaduras.

Allergy	alergia
Chicken pox	varicela
Childhood disease	la enfermedad infantil
Children's hospital	clínica infantil
Cold	el resfriado
Ear infection	otitis media
Fever	la fiebre
Fungal infection	los hongos
German measles	rubeola
Immunization card	el carnet de vacunación
Insect bite	la picadura de insecto
Measles	el sarampión
Medicinal food	los alimentos curativos
Mumps	las paperas
Nosebleed	hemorragia nasal
Pedialyte®	la solución electrolítica
Rash	la erupción
Scarlet fever	escarlatina

Disabilities and obstacles

In recent years, particularly in cities, an effort has been made to improve the situation for people with disabilities: Access ramps have been provided at pedestrian crossings, many buses have lifts or ramps, and access to public buildings has been improved. New or modernized hotels and restaurants, too, have installed special facilities to accommodate people with disabilities.

I am...
Soy...

physically disabled
minusválido.

blind
ciego./ciega.

I cannot walk well. I am lame.
No puedo andar bien. Soy cojo.

I have multiple sclerosis.
Tengo esclerosis múltiple.

Getting Around

Can I take my fold-up wheelchair in the plane with me?
¿Puedo llevar mi propia silla de ruedas plegable en el avión?

Will there be a wheelchair waiting for me when I leave/arrive?
¿Habrá a disposición alguna silla de ruedas a la salida/llegada?

Could I have an aisle seat?
¿Podría tener un asiento en el pasillo?

Is there a restroom for the handicapped?
¿Hay WC/lavabo para minusválidos?

Could somebody help me during the transfer?
¿Podría ayudarme alguien en el transbordo?

Are the doors of the train at ground level?
¿Es plano el acceso a los coches?

Are there buses with wheelchair ramps?
¿Hay autobuses con rampas para minusválidos?

Are there access ramps to the train tracks?
¿Hay rampas que permitan acceder a los andenes con sillas de ruedas?

Do you have rental cars with hand throttles for the handicapped?
¿Se pueden alquilar coches para minusválidos con acelerador manual?

72

Do you rent RVs suitable for wheelchair users?
¿Alquilan ustedes autocaravanas adaptadas a usuarios con sillas de ruedas?

Accommodations

Could you send me information about which hotels in ... are suitable for people with wheelchairs?
¿Podría usted enviarme informaciones sobre hoteles en... que estén preparados para personas con sillas de ruedas?

Could you please tell me which hotels and campgrounds have special facilities for the disabled?
¿Sabría decirme, por favor, qué hoteles y campings disponen de instalaciones adecuadas para minusválidos?

Museums, Sights, Theater ...

Is the exhibition wheelchair-accessible?
¿Los minusválidos pueden llegar a la exposición con ascensores?

Are there city guided tours for deaf people?
¿Hay visitas a la ciudad programadas para sordos?

Are there museum tours/theater performances for deaf mutes/blind people?
¿Se hacen visitas concertadas al museo/representaciones teatrales para sordomudos/ciegos?

Accessibility	la accesibilidad
Ambulatory	ambulatorio
Ascending platform	plataforma ascendente
Association for the disabled	la asociación de minusválidos
At ground level	plano
Automatic door	puerta automática
Automatic door opener	portero electrónico
Barrier-free	sin barreras
Blind	ciego/ciega
Boarding assistance	ayuda para subir
Cabin for wheelchair users	cabina para personas con sillas de ruedas
Cane for the blind	el bastón para ciegos
Completely deaf	completamente sordo
Crutch	muleta
Deaf	sordo/sorda
Deaf mute	sordomudo/sordomuda
Disability	la minusvalidez
Disabled identification card	el carnet de minusválido

Dispensary	dispensario
Door width	ancho de la puerta
Doorstep	el umbral
Epilepsy	epilepsia
Guide	el/la acompañante
Hand throttle (cars)	el acelerador manual
Hand-operated bicycle	bicicleta impulsada con las manos
Handrail	barandilla
Hard of hearing	con sordera
Headphones	el auricular
Height	altura
Help service for the disabled	servicio de ayuda
Holding tape	cinta de sujeción
Incline	subida; la pendiente
Keyboard telephone	teléfono táctil (escrito)
Mute	mudo/muda
Needful of sanitary care	necesitado de cuidados sanitarios
Paraplegic	parapléjico
Psychically handicapped	minusválido psíquico
Ramp	rampa
Ramp	rampa de acceso
Rotary steering wheel knob	el volante adaptado con botón de viraje
Sanitary facilities	los servicios sanitarios
Seeing-eye dog	perro para ciegos
Severely disabled	el/la inválido/inválida
Shower seat	ducha con asiento
Sign language	el lenguaje por señas
Stairs	escalera
Step	peldaño
Suitable for the disabled	adecuado para minusválidos
Transportation service	servicio de transporte
Walk-challenged; lame	con dificultades al andar; cojo
Walking assistance	ayuda para andar
Wheelchair	silla de ruedas
Wheelchair lifter	el elevador para silla de ruedas
Wheelchair user	persona con silla de ruedas
Wheelchair-accessible	accesible para personas con sillas de ruedas
Wheelchair-accessible parking lot	aparcamiento para minusválidos
Wheelchair-accessible restroom	lavabo para minusválidos
Width	ancho

Accommodations

As you make your bed ...

As a popular tourist destination, Spain has an enormous number of hotels and other places to stay. Nevertheless, anyone who plans to vacation in Spain during the summer should make reservations far ahead of time.

The Spaniards take their vacation between mid-July and mid-September, and the peak season is July and August. The prices are noticeably higher in these months.

If you don't want to spend your vacation in the tourist centers, there are attractive alternatives. *Agroturismo,* for example, is growing in popularity. This involves a stay on farms, which usually are located in areas with a beautiful landscape and are especially suitable for children. Frequently they offer their guests products and foods grown or made right on the farm. The *paradores,* too, are something quite special: luxury hotels in unusual—often historic—buildings and in gorgeous settings. Campgrounds in all categories are available on every coast of Spain; in summer they usually are completely full. And keep this in mind: when Spaniards go camping, they are less likely to look for peace and quiet than for fun and social life.

Information

Excuse me, Sir/Madam/Miss, could you recommend...
Perdón, señor/señora/señorita. ¿Podría usted indicarme...

a good hotel?
un buen hotel?

an inexpensive hotel?
un hotel barato?

a guest house?
una pensión?

a bed and breakfast?
una habitación particular?

Is it centrally located/quiet/near the beach?
¿Está en un lugar central/tranquilo/cerca de la playa?

Is there a campground around here?
¿Hay por aquí un camping?

Is there a youth hostel around here?
¿Hay por aquí un albergue juvenil?

Hotel—Pension—Bed-and-Breakfast

At the Reception Desk

I have reserved a room. My name is…
He reservado una habitación. Me llamo…

Do you have any vacancies…
¿Tienen ustedes habitaciones libres…

… for one night?
… para una noche?

… for two days?
… para dos días?

… for a week?
… para una semana?

I am sorry, we do not have.
Lo siento, no tenemos.

Yes. What sort of room would you like?
Sí. ¿Qué clase de habitación desea usted?

I would like…
Quisiera…

a single room.
una habitación individual

a double room.
una habitación doble

a quiet room.
una habitación tranquila

a room with a shower.
una habitación con ducha.

a room with a bathroom.
una habitación con baño.

a room with a balcony.
una habitación con balcón/terraza.

a room with a view of the ocean.
una habitación con vista al mar

a room with/without air conditioning.
una habitación con/sin aire acondicionado.

a room facing the inner courtyard.
una habitación que dé al patio interior.

May I see the room?
¿Puedo ver la habitación?

I don't like this room. Could you show me another, please?
Esta habitación no me gusta. ¿Puede enseñarme otra, por favor?

I will take this room.
Tomaré esta habitación.

Could you put another bed/a bed for a child?
¿Podrían poner otra cama / una cama para un niño?

What does a room cost with...
¿Cuánto cuesta la habitación con...

breakfast?
desayuno?
breakfast and dinner?
media pensión?
all inclusive?
pensión completa?

Will you please fill out the registration form?
¿Quiere hacer el favor de rellenar el formulario de inscripción?

May I see your passport/ID?
¿Puedo ver su pasaporte/carnet de identidad?

Will you please have my luggage brought to the room?
¿Podría encargar que suban mis maletas a la habitación?

Where can I park my car?
¿Dónde puedo aparcar el coche?

In our garage.
En nuestro garaje.

In our parking lot.
En nuestro estacionamiento.

Asking for Service
➢ also Breakfast

At what time is breakfast served?
¿A partir de qué hora se puede desayunar?

When are meals served?
¿A qué hora se sirven las comidas?

Where is the dining room?
¿Dónde está el comedor?

Where is breakfast served?
¿Dónde se sirve el desayuno?

Could you wake me up tomorrow at 7?
¿Me podrían despertar mañana a las 7?

Please wake me up tomorrow at...
Haga el favor de despertarme mañana a las...

Would you please bring...
¿Serían tan amables de traerme...

a towel?
una toalla?
another blanket?
otra manta/otro edredón?

78

Will you please serve breakfast in my room tomorrow?
¿Me hará el favor de servirme mañana el desayuno en la habitación?

How does … work?
¿Cómo funciona…?

Room number 24, please.
Habitación 24, por favor

Are there any letters for me?
¿Hay cartas para mí?

Where can I …
¿Dónde puedo…

  rent a car?
  alquilar un coche?

  make a phone call?
  llamar por teléfono?

Can I leave my valuables in your safe?
¿Puedo depositar mis objetos de valor en su caja de seguridad?

May I leave my luggage here?
¿Puedo dejar las maletas aquí?

Complaints

My room has not been cleaned today.
Hoy no han limpiado la habitación.

The air conditioning doesn't work.
El aire acondicionado no funciona.

The faucet leaks.
El grifo del agua gotea.

There is no (hot) water.
No sale agua (caliente).

The toilet/sink is plugged up.
El wáter / El lavabo está atascado (*Am* tapado).

Departure

I'll be leaving this evening / tomorrow at…
Me marcho esta tarde / mañana a las…

When do I have to check out?
¿A qué hora tengo que dejar libre la habitación?

Could you prepare the bill please?
Prepáreme la cuenta, por favor.

Do you take credit cards?
¿Aceptan ustedes tarjetas de crédito?

Could you please call a taxi for me?
¿Puede pedirme un taxi, por favor?

Thank you very much for everything. Good-bye.
Muchas gracias por todo. Adiós.

Adapter	el enchufe intermedio
Admission	la recepción
All inclusive (full room and board)	la pensión completa
Armchair	el sillón
Ash tray	cenicero
Balcony	el balcón
Bath towel	toalla para el baño
Bathroom	cuarto de baño
Bathtub	bañera, baño
Bed	cama
Bed linen	ropa de cama
Bidet	bidé
Blanket	colcha; (wollen) manta
Breakfast	desayuno
Breakfast buffet	el bufete libre (para desayunar)
Breakfast included	media pensión
Breakfast room	sala de desayuno
Chair	silla
Clean	limpio
Clean, to	limpiar
Closet	armario
Coat hanger	percha
Cup	taza
Dining room	el comedor
Dinner	cena
Electrical outlet	el enchufe, caja de enchufe
Elevator	el ascensor
Extended week	semana de prórroga
Fan	el ventilador
Faucet	grifo (*Am* canilla)
Fix, to	arreglar
Floor	piso
Garage	el garaje
Garbage can	cubo de la basura
Glass	vaso
Hall	el hall
Hand-held shower	ducha de teléfono
Heating	la calefacción
Housekeeper	camarera (del hotel)
Key	la llave

Lamp	lámpara
Laundry charge	cambio de ropa
Light switch	el interruptor, la llave de la luz
Lightbulb	bombilla
Lunch	comida, almuerzo
Mattress	el colchón
Mirror	espejo
Night table	mesita de noche
Notebook	libreta
Off season	temporada baja
Overnight stay	la pernoctación
Parking	el parking, aparcamiento
Peak season	temporada alta
Pillow	almohada
Place setting	cubierto (para el desayuno)
Plug	clavija de enchufe
Porter	portero
Price list *(for example, for the mini-bar)*	lista de precios
Reading lamp	lámpara de mesita de noche
Reservation	reserva
Restrooms	los servicios, baño
Room	la habitación *(Am pieza)*
Safe	caja de caudales , caja fuerte
Shoe polish	material para limpiar zapatos
Shower	ducha
Shower curtain/ shower slider	cortina de la ducha/mampara corredera
Showerhead	la roseta de la ducha
Shuttle bus	el autobús/microbús del/al aeropuerto
Sink	lavabo
Stationery	el papel de cartas
Table	mesa
Telephone in the room	teléfono de la habitación
Television lounge	sala de televisión
Television set	el televisor
Terrace	terraza
Toilet paper	el papel higiénico
Towel	toalla
Water	(el) agua
cold water	(el) agua fría
hot water	(el) agua caliente
Window	ventana

Vacation Cottages and Apartments

Is electricity/water included in the rental price?
¿Está incluido en el alquiler el precio de la electricidad/del agua?

Are pets allowed?
¿Admiten ustedes animales domésticos?

Where are the garbage cans?
¿Dónde están los cubos de la basura?

Do we have to clean the place before we leave?
¿Tenemos que encargarnos nosotros de la limpieza final?

➢ also Hotel—Pension—Bed-and-Breakfast

Additional expenses	los gastos adicionales
Apartment	apartamento (*Am* departamento)
Bedroom	dormitorio
Bungalow	el bungalow
Bunk beds	las literas
Central heating	la calefacción central
Coffeemaker	cafetera
Day of arrival	el día de llegada
Dish towel	paño de cocina
Dishes	vajilla
Dishwasher	el lavaplatos, el lavavajillas
Electricity	la corriente, la electricidad
Farm	granja
Final cleanup	limpieza final
Garbage	basura
Kitchenette	el rincón-cocina
Living room	cuarto de estar
Lump sum for electricity	tarifa global de electricidad
Owner	dueño de la casa
Pets	los animales domésticos
Refrigerator	nevera
Rent	el alquiler
Rent, to	alquilar
Resort	el lugar de temporada
Returning the keys	entrega de las llaves
Sofabed	el sofá-cama
Stove	cocina
Electric stove	cocina eléctrica
Gas stove	cocina de gas
Vacation home	casa de vacaciones
Washing machine	lavadora
Water consumption	consumo de agua

82

Could you tell me where the nearest campground is?
¿Podría decirme si hay por aquí cerca un camping?

Is there space for a trailer home/a tent?
¿Tienen ustedes sitio para una caravana (*Am* una casa rodante) / una tienda (*Am* una carpa)?

How much does it cost per day and per person?
¿Cuánto cuesta por día y por persona?

What is the charge for...
¿Cuánto se paga por...

a car?
un coche?

a trailer home?
una caravana (*Am* una casa rodante)?

an RV?
una autocaravana?

a tent?
una tienda de campaña?

Do you rent trailer homes?
¿Alquilan ustedes caravanas?

We plan to stay ... days/weeks.
Pensamos quedarnos... días/semanas.

Where are...
¿Dónde están...

the restrooms?
los servicios?

the washrooms?
los lavabos?

the showers?
las duchas?

Is there electricity here?
¿Hay aquí corriente eléctrica?

Where can I exchange my gas cylinder?
¿Dónde puedo cambiar botellas de butano (*Am* garrafas de gas)?

Camp, to	acampar, hacer camping
Campground	el terreno de camping
Camping	el camping
Camping guide	guía de campings
Camping ID	el carnet de campista
Drinking water	(el) agua potable
Electric plug	clavija de enchufe
Electrical outlet	toma de corriente

ACCOMMODATIONS

83

Electricity	la corriente, la electricidad
Gas camping stove	horno de gas
Gas cartridge	cartucho de gas
Gas cylinder	bombona (*Am* garrafa) de gas
Kerosene lamp	lámpara de petróleo
Lavatories	los lavabos
Propane/butane gas	el gas propano/butano
Reservation	aviso previo
RV	autocaravana
Sink	fregadero
Sleeping bag	saco de dormir (*Am* bolsa de dormir)
Stove	hornillo, horno
Tent	tienda de campaña (*Am* carpa)
Tent peg	el piquete
Tent pole	palo de tienda de campaña
Tent rope	cuerda de tienda de campaña
Toilet	inodoro, excusado
Trailer home	caravana (*Am* casa rodante)
Water	(el) agua
Water jug	el bidón (*Am* el tanque)

A COMER BIEN
Y BARATO
SAN MILLAN 4

F. BLANCO

Bon appétit!

Spain's cuisine is both delicious and full of variety: excellent seafood, surprising meat dishes, and vegetables of a great many kinds. In addition, the wines are good and quite affordable. Each region has its own cuisine with tasty specialties that you definitely should sample:

Andalusia:	*gazpacho andaluz* (cold soup made of puréed raw vegetables)
Balearic Islands:	*caldereta de pescado* {fish stew}
Basque country:	*bacalao a la vasca* (cod with red sauce)
	besugo al horno (baked sea bream)
Galicia:	fish, seafood, oysters
Catalonia:	*fabes a la catalana* (fava beans with mint, paprika sausage, and wine)
Northern Castile:	*cordero al horno* (oven-roasted leg of lamb)
	olla podrida (stew containing mean, chickpeas, bacon, and vegetables)
Valencia:	*paella valenciana* (rice dish with chicken, beans, and seafood)

Terms for places to eat in Spain

el café is roughly equivalent to a small American coffee shop café, but in the past few years the café has been replaced in many cases by **cafeterías,** where coffee, beverages, or alcohol can be drunk. Cakes and pastries are not always available, however.

el bar is a place where you can get everything from coffee to alcoholic beverages and also have a little snack.

la cafetería is an establishment in which you can order drinks of all kinds, Spain's typical appetizers (*tapas*), and small meals at the bar, at a table, or on the terrace.

la taberna (popularly known as **tasca**) is a relatively small place where you can drink and purchase primarily wine, but other beverages as well.

el (café-)restaurante is a relatively large place where you can get something to drink and eat lunch or dinner.

el chiringuito is an outdoor cafe, almost always at the beach, that is open during peak season and serves beverages and mainly fish dishes.

la hamburguesería is a fast-food restaurant where primarily hamburgers (*hamburguesas*), beverages, french fries, and the like are served.

Is there … here?
¿Dónde hay por aquí cerca…

a good restaurant
un buen restaurante?

an inexpensive restaurant
un restaurante no demasiado caro?

a fast-food restaurant
un restaurante (de servicio) rápido?

Where can I eat well/inexpensively around here?
¿Dónde se puede comer bien/por poco dinero por aquí cerca?

At the Restaurant

We would like to reserve a table for four for this evening?
¿Puede reservarnos para esta noche una mesa para cuatro personas?

Is this table/seat taken?
¿Está ocupada esta mesa/este asiento?

A table for two/three, please.
Una mesa para dos/tres personas, por favor.

Where are the restrooms, please?
¿Dónde están los servicios, por favor?

Do you mind if I smoke?
¿Puedo fumar?

Lunch, eaten between 1 and 4 P.M., is the main meal of the day in Spain. Most stores are closed during these hours. In the evening, restaurants generally are open from 8 P.M. to 12 A.M. It is customary to order two courses. If you order the daily special (two courses plus bread and dessert), you normally will be served a beverage—water, wine, or beer—whose cost is included in the price. The daily special is priced at 7 euros and up. Lunch in Latin America is closer to American customs regarding hours and portions. Dining hours vary according to the size and sophistication of the city.

EATING AND DRINKING

Excuse me...
Disculpe...

the menu.
la carta (*Am* el menú).

the wine list please.
La carta de vinos, por favor.

What can you recommend?
¿Qué me recomienda usted?

Do you serve vegetarian/low-fat meals?
¿Tienen ustedes comida vegatariana/dietética?

Do you also serve children's meals?
¿Hacen ustedes también platos especiales para niños?

Are you ready to order?
¿Ya han elegido?

I'll have...
Voy a tomar...

I'll have the ... as an appetizer/as an entrée/for desert.
Voy a tomar de primer plato / de segundo / de postres...

No appetizer for me, thank you.
Yo no tomo primer plato, gracias.

I'm afraid we are out of the...
Lo lamento, pero ya no tenemos...

This meal should be ordered in advance.
Esta comida hay que encargarla por anticipado.

Could I have ... instead of ...?
¿Puede traerme... en lugar de...?

I am allergic to ... .Could you make this dish without ...?
... no me sienta bien. ¿Puede prepararme la comida sin...?

How would you like your steak?
¿Como desea usted el filete?

well-done
bien pasado

medium rare
poco pasado

rare
a la inglesa

What would you like to drink?
¿Qué desea beber (*Am* tomar)?

A glass of ..., please.
Un vaso de..., por favor.

A bottle of …/Half a bottle of …, please.
Una botella / Media botella de…, por favor.

With ice, please.
Con hielo, por favor.

Enjoy! (your food)
¡Que aproveche!

Cheers!
¡Salud!

Would you like anything else?
¿Desea usted algo más?

Could you bring us …, please?
Tráiganos…, por favor.

Could you please bring us some more bread/water/wine?
¿Puede traernos un poco más de pan/agua/vino?

Complaints

We need (another) …
Aquí falta un… / una…

Have you forgotten my …?
¿Se ha olvidado usted de mi…?

I didn't order this.
Yo no he pedido esto.

The soup is cold/too salty.
La sopa está fría/salada.

The meat is tough/has too much fat.
La carne está dura / tiene demasiada grasa.

The fish is not fresh.
El pescado no es fresco.

Please take it away.
Lléveselo, por favor.

Please call the manager.
Llame al dueño, por favor.

The Bill

If you go to a restaurant with friends, it is customary to share the costs for the entire meal.

The check, please!
¡La cuenta, por favor!

All on one check, please.
Todo junto, por favor.

Separate checks, please.
Cuentas separadas, por favor.

Is service included?
¿Está el servicio incluido?

There seems to be a mistake on the check.
Me parece que hay un error en la cuenta.

I didn't have that. I had …
Esto no me lo ha servido. Yo tenía…

"Did you enjoy your meal?"
You'll never be asked this question in a Spanish restaurant—
but of course you're free to praise the kitchen as much as you
like.

The food was excellent.
La comida estaba excelente.

Keep the change.
Está bien así.

In Spain, leaving a tip is not obligatory, but it is viewed as the
usual thing to do in restaurants. The amount of the tip is left
to your discretion. If you want to tip, simply place the money
on the saucer on which the bill was presented. Now you can
leave without having to wait for the waiter to return.
In Latin America tips are a must… unless the establishment
adds the tip on its own. Check your check to see if the
propina (tip) is included.

Cafés and Bars

It's not customary to take a seat at tables that are already
occupied, even if these are the only vacant seats in the entire
place. This applies especially to restaurants.

What would you like to drink?
¿Qué desea tomar?

A draft beer, please.
Una cerveza de barril, por favor.

A mug or a glass?
¿Una jarra o una caña?

A glass, please.
Una caña, por favor.

Red wine, please.
Un vino tinto, por favor.

I would like a black coffee/a latte, please
Quisiera un café solo / un café con leche, por favor.

One more, please.
Otro, por favor.

What kind of food do you have?
¿Qué tiene para comer?

We have hors d'oeuvres, and appetizers also.
Tenemos bocadillos y también tapas.

I pay this round.
Esta ronda la pago yo.

Cheers! To your health! *(only on festive occasions)*
¡Salud! / ¡A tu/su salud!

Gentlemen, we are closing.
Señores, vamos a cerrar.

tapas	Appetizers
sangría	Sangria
moscatel	Muscatel
una clara (cerveza con limonada)	Clara (beer with lemonade)
chocolate con churros	Chocolate (hot) with churros
granizado de limón/café	Iced lemon beverage
café solo	Espresso
cortado	Espresso with milk
café con leche	Coffee latte
café con hielo	Iced coffee
horchata de chufa	Milk with almonds
helado de turrón	Nougat ice cream
batido	Milkshake
té	Tea
Té verde	Green tea
Bolsita de té	Teabag
Leche con plátano	Banana milkshake

91

➢ also Groceries

Appetizers	el primer plato, los entremeses
Ashtray	cenicero
Be hungry, to	tener hambre
Bone	hueso
Breakfast	desayuno
Carafe	garrafa
Children's meal	plato infantil
Coffee	café
Cook	cocinero
Corkscrew	el sacacorchos
Course	plato
Cutlery	los cubiertos
Dessert	el postre
Diabetic	diabético
Diet	dieta
Dinner	cena
Dish	plato, comida; la fuente
Drink	bebida
Dry (wine)	seco
Entrée	comida principal
Fishbone	espina
Fork	el tenedor
Fried food	comida a la sartén
Glass	vaso
Tumbler, glass	vaso para agua
Wine glass	vaso para vino
Hard boiled (egg)	duro
Homemade	casero
Hot	(muy) caliente
Ketchup	el ketchup
Knife	cuchillo
Lunch	comida, almuerzo
Mayonnaise	mayonesa
Menu	carta (*Am* el menú)
Mustard	mostaza
Napkin	servilleta
Non-alcoholic	sin alcohol

Oil	el aceite
On tap	de barril
Order	pedido
Pepper	pimienta
Pepper shaker	pimentero
Place setting	cubierto
Portion	la ración
Roast	parrilla
Saccharine	sacarina
Salad bar	el bufete de ensaladas diversas
Salad dressing	aliño
Salt	la sal
Salt shaker	salero
Sauce	salsa
Saucer	taza
Plate	plato pequeño
Season, to	sazonar
Seasoning	especia, condimento
Server	camarero/camarera
Slice	*(bread)* rebanada; *(meat)* tajada; *(sausage)* rodaja
Soup	sopa
Soup bowl	plato de sopa
Specialty	la especialidad
Spoon	cuchara
Teaspoon	cucharilla
Stain	mancha
Straw	pajita
Sugar	el azúcar
Sweet	dulce
Tablecloth	el mantel
Tea	té
Teller	plato
Tip	propina
Today's special	plato del día
Toothpick	palillo (de dientes)
Vegetarian	vegetariano
Vinegar	el vinagre
Waiter	camarero
Water	(el) agua

Preparation

au gratin	gratinado
baked	frito
bitter	agrio
braised	estofado
cooked	cocido
done	en su punto, bien cocido/asado
hard	duro
hot (spicy)	picante
juicy	jugoso
lean	magro
raw	crudo
roasted	asado
fried	en la sartén
grilled	a la parrilla
spit-roasted	en el asador
smoked	ahumado
soft	blando
steamed	al vapor
stuffed	relleno
sweet	dulce
tender	tierno
toasted	tostado
well-done	bien asado

boiled
hervido

cooked
cocido

steamed
al vapor

double boiler
(bain marie)
al baño María

roasted
asado

fried
frito

grilled
al grill

I would like ...
quisiera...

Ginger jengibre

Garlic
ajo

Onion
cebolla

Dill
eneldo

Bay leaf
laurel

Rosemary
romero

Majoram/Oregano
mejorana/orégano

Cilantro
cilantro

Parsley
perejil

Basil
albahaca

96

Nutmeg nuez moscada

Hot peppers
chile

Pepperoni
guindilla
verde

Chives
cebollino

Sage
salvia

Chervil
perifollo

Thyme
tomillo

Savory
ajedrea de jardín

Lovage
levística

97

I would like ...
Quisiera...

I would like ...

Quisiera...

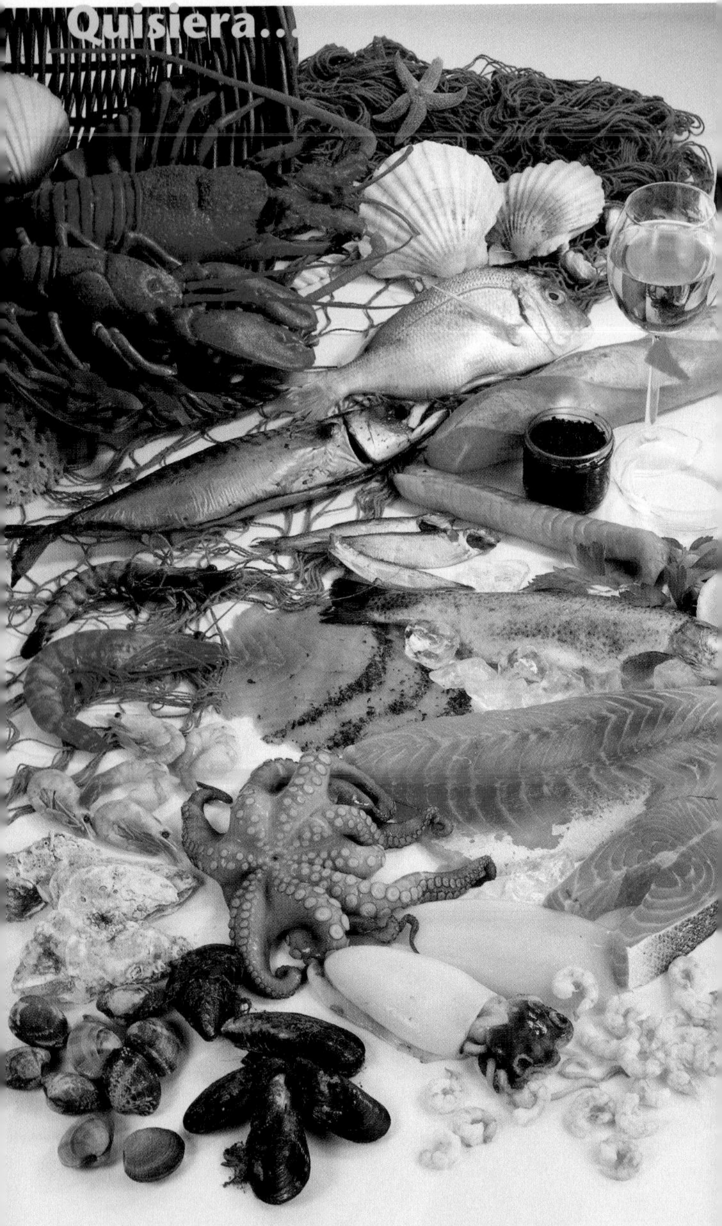

In general, breakfast is a very light meal in Spain. Later in the morning people drink coffee with milk or espresso in a bar or cafeteria and eat a pastry (*pasta*) with it.
In Latin America breakfast is more generous, although it seldom includes American ham-and-eggs levels.

Desayuno	Breakfast
café solo	Black coffee
café con leche	Coffee with milk
café descafeinado	Decaffeinated coffee
té con leche/limón	Tea with milk
infusión (manzanilla, menta, tila...)	Herbal tea (chamomile, peppermint, etc.)
cacao	Cocoa
zumo de fruta	Fruit juice
huevo pasado por agua	Soft-boiled egg
huevos revueltos	Scrambled eggs
huevos con bacon	Eggs with bacon
pan/panecillo/tostada	Bread/roll/toast
croissant	Croissant
mantequilla	Butter
queso	Cheese
embutido	Sausage
jamón (serrano/york)	Ham (dry/cooked)
miel	Honey
mermelada	Marmelade
cereales	Cereals
yogur	Yoghurt
fruta	Fruit

Tourist menu	
Ensalada	Salad
Canalones de berenjenas con gambas	Eggplant and shrimp rollatini
Bacalao al ajillo	Codfish in garlic sauce
Postre: helado, yogurt o tarta de chocolate	Dessert: ice-cream, yoghurt or chocolate cake
Consomé	Consommé

Chuleta de ternera con patatas y guisantes	Veal cutlet with potatoes and peas
Postre (flan o fruta del tiempo) o café	Dessert (baked custard o seasonal fruit) or coffee
Gazpacho	Gazpacho soup (oil, tomatoes, vinegar, salt, garlic, onions, and bread—served cold)
Pechuga de pollo o Merluza	Chicken breast or hake
Fruta del tiempo	Fruit in season

Entrantes	Hors d'oeuvres
aceitunas	Olives
alcachofas	Artichokes
almejas	Mussels
boquerones	Sardines (small)
buñuelos de bacalao	Codfish cakes
cangrejos	Crabs
caracoles	Snails
croquetas	Croquettes
chorizo	Sausage
embutido	Cold cut
ensaladilla rusa	Russian salad (potato salad with eggs, peas, pickles, carrots, and mayonnaise)
fiambre	Cold meats
gambas	Shrimp
gambas al ajillo	Shrimp in garlic sauce
gambas a la plancha	Grilled shrimp
jamón serrano	Dry ham
jamón (de) york	Cooked ham
mejillones	Mussels
salchichón	Salami
salpicón de marisco	Cold shellfish hash
sardinas	Sardines (large)

Sopas	Soups
caldo	Bouillon
consomé	Consommé
crema de espárragos	Creamed asparagus
fabada asturiana	Bean and bacon soup
gazpacho	Gazpacho (oil, tomatoes, vinegar, salt, garlic, onions, and bread—served cold)

sopa de ajo	Garlic soup
sopa de arroz	Rice soup
sopa de fideos	Noodle soup
sopa de pescado	Fish soup
sopa de verduras (juliana, jardinera)	Vegetable soup

Pescados y Mariscos — Fish and shellfish

anguila	Eel
angulas	Elver
arenque	Herring
atún	Tuna
bacalao	Cod
besugo	Red porgy
bogavante	Lobster
bonito	Striped tuna
caballa	Mackerel
calamar	Squid
pejerrey	Atherine (variety of mackerel)
carpa	Carp
centollo	Spider crab
tiburón	shark
corvina	Corbina
dorada	Gilthead
gambas	Shrimp
langosta	Lobster
langostinos	Crawfish
lenguado	Sole
lubina	Sea bass
merluza	Hake
paella	Paella (rice dish with meat, fish, or seafood and vegetables) *(see also Meat)*
parrillada de pescado	Grilled fish
perca	Perch
pescadilla	Whiting
pez espada	Swordfish
platija	Plaice
pulpo	Octopus
rape	Angler
raya	Ray
rodaballo	Brill
salmón	Salmon
salmonete	Red mullet

congrio	Conger eel
trucha	Trout
lenguado	Flounder

Carnes y Aves	**Meat and poultry**
asado	Roast meat
bistec	Steak
cabrito	Kid
callos	Tripe
carne picada	Chopped meat
carne de vaca	Beef
cerdo	Pork
cocido	Cooked
cochinillo	Suckling pig
conejo	Rabbit
cordero	Lamb
cordero lechal	Suckling lamb
chuleta (*Am* costeleta)	Chop
empanada	Meat pie
escalope	Scaloppini
estofado	Stew
faisán	Pheasant
filete	Fillet
guisado	Casserole dish
hígado	Liver
lengua	Tongue
liebre	Hare
lomo	Saddle
paella	Paella (rice dish with meat, fish, or seafood and vegetables) *(see also Fish)*
parrillada de carne	Grilled meat
pato	Duck
pavo	Turkey
perdiz	Partridge
pechuga de pollo	Chicken breast
pichón	Squab
pollo	Chicken
riñones	Kidneys
rosbif	Roast beef
sesos	Brains
solomillo	Sirloin
ternera	Veal

Ensalada y Verduras	Salads and vegetables
acelgas	Chard
alcachofas	Artichokes
berenjenas	Eggplant
cebollas	Onions
col de Bruselas	Brussels sprouts
coliflor	Cauliflower
ensalada variada/mixta	Mixed salad
apio	Celery
escarola	Endive
espárragos	Asparagus
garbanzos	Chickpea
guisantes	Pea
judías blancas (alubias)	Kidney beans
judías verdes	Green beans
lentejas	Lentils
lechuga	Lettuce
patatas (*Am* papas)	Potatoes
patatas (*Am* papas) fritas	French fries
pepino	Cucumber
pimiento	Pepper
pisto (manchego)	Pesto
setas	Mushrooms
tomate	Tomato
zanahorias	Carrots

Platos de huevos	Egg dishes
huevos con jamón	ham and eggs
huevos duros	Hard-boiled eggs
huevos fritos	Fried eggs
huevos pasados por agua	Soft-boiled eggs
huevos revueltos	Scrambled eggs
tortilla (a la) española	Spanish omelet (eggs with potatoes)
huevos con tocino	bacon and eggs

Postres, queso y fruta	Desserts, cheese and fruit
albaricoques (*Am* damascos)	Apricot
arroz con leche	Rice pudding
cerezas	Cherries
ciruelas	Plums
compota	Compote
flan	Flan
fresas (*Am* frutilla)	Strawberries
higos	Figs
macedonia de frutas	Fruit salad
mandarina	Mandarin
manzana	Apple
melocotón (*Am* durazno)	Peach
melón	Mellon
naranja	Orange
natillas	Custard
pera	Pear
piña (*Am* ananás)	Pineapple
plátano (*Am* banana)	Banana
queso de cabra	Goat cheese
queso (de) Gruyère	Gruyere
queso manchego	Manchego cheese
queso de oveja	Sheep cheese
requesón	Cottage cheese
sandía	Watermelon
tarta	Tart, pastry
toronja	Grapefruit
uvas	Grapes

Helados	Ice cream
café con hielo	Ice coffee
copa de helado	Ice cream cup
copa de helado con frutas	Ice cream with fruit
helado de chocolate	Chocolate ice cream
helado de fresa	Strawberry ice cream
helado de limón	Lemon ice cream
helado de vainilla	Vanilla ice cream
helado de coco	Coconut ice cream
mantecado	Milkshake
sorbete de limón	Lemon sherbet

Dulces	Sweets
bombón	Bonbon
chocolate	Chocolate
churros	Crullers
crema catalana	Caramel-vanilla pudding
dulces	Sweets
galletas	Cookies
nata	Custard
nata batida/montada	Whipped cream
pastas, pasteles	Baked sweets
pastelillos de crema	Cream pastry
pastel	Pie
tarta	Tart
tarta de crema	Cream tart
tarta helada	Ice tart
tarta de frutas	Fruit tart
tarta de manzana	Apple tart
torta	Cake
turrón	Nougat
dulce de leche	Caramel
caramelo	Hard candy

Turrón is traditionally made of almonds and honey. Today there are many other varieties. Most **turrones** come from the region of Valencia, where they have been known since the thirteenth century.

Bebidas   Drinks

Vinos típicos españoles y latinoamericanos
Typical Spanish and Latin American wines

Cariñena	aromatic sweet wine from Saragossa
Chacolí	light dry wine of Northern Spain
Jerez dulce/oloroso	sweet sherry
Málaga	sweet wine, originally from Malaga
Manzanilla	pale dry sherry
Montilla	white wine aperitif
Vino añejo	strong sweet wine
Moscatel	muscatel
Priorato	red wine from Catalonia
Casillero del Diablo	strong red wine from Chile
Rioja	dry red or white wine
Sangría	sangria (wine and fruit drink)
Valdepeñas	fine red wine

Otras bebidas alcohólicas   Other spirits

aguardiente	firewater, brandy
anís	anisette
caña de cerveza	draft beer
cerveza light	light beer
coñac	cognac
cuba libre	Coca-Cola with rum
champán	Champagne
ginebra	Gin
licor	Liqueur
sidra	Cider
vodka	Vodka

Sidra is a sparkling wine made from apples. It has a low alcohol content (5-7%) and a slightly sour taste. It is especially popular in Asturias (northern Spain).

EATING AND DRINKING

Bebidas no alcohólicas	Nonalcoholic drinks
agua mineral (con gas/sin gas)	Mineral water (with or without gas)
batido	Malt
cacao	Cocoa
(café) americano	Large black coffee
café solo	Espresso
café con leche	Coffee latte
(café) cortado	Espresso with a dash of milk
(café) descafeinado	Decaffeinated coffee
gaseosa	Soda
horchata	Orgeat (beverage made from barley and almonds)
leche	Milk
limonada	Lemonade
naranjada	Orangeade
agua de Seltz	Seltzer
té	Tea
(agua) tónica	Tonic water
zumo (*Am* jugo) de fruta	Fruit juice
zumo (*Am* jugo) de limón, limón natural	Lemon juice
zumo (*Am* jugo) de naranja	Orange juice

Take a look!

In Madrid:	National museum *El Prado*: most important collection of Spanish painting of the sixteenth through eighteenth centuries (El Greco, Velázquez, Goya, and others), but also shows works of foreign painters with an international reputation (Rubens, Brueghel, Tizian, and others)
	Reina Sofía art center: museum of contemporary art, with the emphasis on Spanish painting and sculpture of the twentieth century (Picasso, Gris, Dalí, Miró, and others)
	Thyssen-Bornemisza Museum: Private collection with paintings from the fourteenth through twentieth centuries (Dürer, Mondrian, Juan Gris, and others)
In Barcelona:	*Palau Nacional:* Catalan art from the romantic period to the present day, as well as works by El Greco, Velázquez, Tàpies, and others)
	Joan Miró Foundation: Collection of Joan Miró with paintings, prints, sculpture, and so forth from all his phases of creativity, as well as works by Braque, Calder, Tàpies, and others
In Figueras (near Gerona):	*Dalí Theater-Museum:* A great many of Dalí's works are exhibited in his home town
In Bilbao:	*Guggenheim Museum:* Architecturally striking museum for modern and contemporary art of the twentieth century, as well as a convention center

At the Tourist Information Office

I would like a map of...
Quisiera un mapa de...

Do you have a schedule of events for this week?
¿Tienen ustedes un programa de espectáculos para esta semana?

Are there sightseeing tours of the city?
¿Hay visitas organizadas de la ciudad?

How much does the ticket cost, please?
¿Cuánto cuesta el billete (*Am* boleto), por favor?

Places of Interest—Museums

Opening Hours, Guided Tours, Admission

What places of interest there are here?
¿Qué cosas dignas de verse hay aquí?

You really have to see the...
Tiene que visitar sin falta...

At what hours is the museum open?
¿A qué horas está abierto el museo?

When does the guided tour start?
¿A qué hora comienza la visita guiada?

Is there a tour conducted in English?
¿Hay una presentación en inglés?

Are we allowed to take pictures here?
¿Se pueden tomar fotografías aquí?

Two tickets, please.
Dos entradas, por favor.

Two adults and one child.
Dos adultos y un niño.

Are there price discounts for...
¿Se hacen descuentos para...

...children?
... niños?

...students?
... estudiantes?

...senior citizens?
... jubilados?

...groups?
... grupos?

Is there an exhibition catalog?
¿Hay un catálogo de la exposición?

Sightseeing Questions

Is this...?
¿Es éste el... / ¿Es ésta la...?

When was this building built/restored?
¿Cuándo se construyó/restauró este edificio?

Who's this picture by?
¿Quién ha pintado este cuadro?

Do you have a poster/postcard/slide of this?
¿Tiene usted este cuadro en póster/postal/diapositiva?

General

Art	el arte
Birthplace	lugar de nacimiento
City tour/sightseeing	visita de la ciudad, las excursiones
Downtown	centro
Emperor/empress	el emperador/la emperatriz
Finds	hallazgos
Folk museum	museo del folclore
Guide	el/la guía (turístico)
Guided tour	visita guiada
Historical preservation	la protección de los monumentos
History	historia
House	casa
King/queen	el rey/la reina
Landmark	el emblema, símbolo
Lane	callejuela
Market	mercado
Monuments, places of interest	los monumentos, las lugares de interés
Museum	museo
Neighborhood	barrio
Park	el parque
Pedestrian zone	zona peatonal
Pilgrimage	la peregrinación
Prince/princess	el príncipe/la princesa
Reconstruct, to	reconstruir
Religion	la religión
Remains/ruins	restos, ruinas
Restore, to	restaurar
Street	la calle
Suburb	barrio periférico, suburbio
Tour	visita

Architecture

Abbey	abadía
Altar	el altar
Amphitheater	anfiteatro
Arcades	arcada
Arch	arco
Archeology	arqueología
Architect	arquitecto
Architecture	arquitectura
Bridge	el puente
Building	edificio
Bullring	plaza de toros
Castle	castillo, palacio

Cathedral	la catedral
Ceiling	techo
Cemetery	cementerio
Chapel	capilla
Church	iglesia
City hall	ayuntamiento
Cloister	claustro
Column	columna, el pilar
Crypt	cripta
Dome	cúpula
Excavations	las excavaciones
Façade, front	fachada
Fortress	fortaleza, ciudadela
Fountain	la fuente
Gable	frontispicio
Gate	puerta, el portón
Historical district	la ciudad vieja
Hospital	hospital
Indoor market	mercado (cubierto)
Inner courtyard	patio interior
Inscription	la inscripción
Mausoleum	mausoleo
Memorial	el lugar conmemorativo
Monastery	monasterio, convento
Monument	monumento
Obelisk	obelisco
Opera	ópera
Ornamental	ornamental
Palace	palacio
Pavilion	el pabellón
Pilgrimage temple	templo de peregrinación
Portal	el portal
Pulpit	púlpito
Rebuild, to	reconstruir
Roof	tejado
Ruin	ruina
Skyscraper	rascacielos
Square	plaza
Steeple	la torre, campanario
Temple	templo
Theater	teatro
Tomb	tumba
Tower	la torre
Town wall	las murallas (de la ciudad)
Triumphal arch	arco de triumfo
University	la universidad

Vault	bóveda
Wall	muro, la pared
Window	ventana
Wing	(el) ala

Visual Arts

Arts and crafts	las artes industriales, oficio artístico
Bronze	el bronce
Ceramics	cerámica
Copy	copia
Cross	la cruz
Crucifix	crucifijo
Drawing	dibujo
Engraving	grabado
Etching	el aguafuerte
Exhibit	objeto expuesto
Exhibition	la exposición
Gallery	galería
Glass painting	pintura sobre cristal
Gold work	orfebrería
Graphic art	arte gráfico
Lithography	litografía
Model	modelo
Mosaic	mosaico
Nude	desnudo
Original	el original
Painter	el pintor/pintora
Painting	pintura, cuadro
Photography	fotografía
Picture	pintura, cuadro
Porcelain	porcelana
Portrait	retrato
Poster	el cartel
Pottery	alfarería
Sculptor	el escultor
Sculpture	escultura, las artes plásticas
Silkscreen printing	serigrafía
Statue	estatua
Still life	naturaleza muerta, el bodegón
Terra-cotta	terracota, barro cocido
Torso	torso
Vase	florero, el jarrón
Watercolor	acuarela
Woodcarving	talla (en madera)

Styles and Periods

Ancient	antiguo
Arab	árabe
Baroque	barroco
Bronze age	la edad del bronce
Byzantine	bizantino
Century	siglo
Christianity	cristianismo
Cistercian	cisterciense
Classicism	clasicismo
Contemporary	contemporáno
Cubism	cubismo
Dynasty	dinastía
Elizabethan	estilo isabelino
Expressionism	expresionismo
Gothic	gótico
Greek	griego
Heyday	apogeo
Iberian	ibero
Impressionism	impresionismo
Judaism	judaísmo
Latin	latino
Mannerism	manierismo
Middle ages	la Edad Media
Modern	moderno
Modernism	modernismo
Mozarabic	mozárabe
Mudejar style	estilo mudéjar
Pagan	pagano
Period	época
Prehistoric	prehistórico
Renaissance	renacimiento, época renacentista
Rococo	rococó
Romanesque	románico
Romantic	romántico
Stone age	la edad de piedra
Style	estilo
Surrealism	surrealismo
Visigothic	visigótico

Excursions

Where do we leave from?
¿De dónde salimos?

When should we meet?
¿Cuándo nos encontramos?

Will we pass by...?
¿Pasamos por...?

Are we also going to see...?
¿Visitamos también...?

When are we going back?
¿Cuándo regresamos?

Amusement park	el parque de atracciones
Animal sanctuary	reserva de animales
Bird sanctuary	reserva ornitológica
Botanical garden	el jardín botánico
Cave	cueva
Dam	el dique
Day trip	la excursión de un día
Defile	desfiladero, barranco
Departure	salida
Dripstone cave	cueva de estalactitas y estalagmitas
Excursion	la excursión
Fishing port	puerto de pescadores
Fishing town	el lugar de pesca
Forest	el bosque
Forest fire	incendio forestal
Grotto	gruta
Hinterland	zona interior, el interior del país
Lake	lago
Lava	lava
Lookout point	el mirador, punto de observación
Market	mercado
Mountain range	cordillera
Mountain village	pueblo de montaña
National park	el parque nacional
Observatory	observatorio astronómico
Open-air museum	museo al aire libre
Pass	pasaje
Peak	pico
Pilgrimage, place of	el lugar de peregrinación
Reef	escollo
Scenery	el paisaje
Surroundings	los alrededores
Tour (guided) around the island	visita (guiada) de la isla
Valley	el valle
Volcano	el volcán
Waterfall	catarata, cascada
Wilderness area, nature reserve	reserva natural/ecológica
Zoo	el zoo, el parque zoológico

Active Vacations

Beaches for every taste

Spain is a paradise for those who love the beach. There are beaches for every taste: the big waves of the Atlantic, the "wild coast" (*Costa Brava*) of northern Catalonia, the mild temperatures of the Mediterranean, and the volcanic coasts of the Canary Islands. You can get everything you want in the immediate vicinity of the beaches, all the way from a diving mask to a festively set table.

At the easily accessible places, the beaches usually are very crowded. But if you venture a bit farther, you'll find a quiet place to relax. Nude beaches are rare in Spain. If you want to spend your vacation doing something besides loafing, you might consider sailing off Mallorca, surfing off Tarifa, diving off the Illes Medes and Menorca, skiing in the Pyrenees and the Sierra Nevada, an arts-and-crafts vacation in the Alpujarras, golf and horseback riding in Andalusia, extreme sports in the Pyrenees, and hiking in the numerous national parks.

Beaches in Latin America vary from tropical (Central America) through mild (Brazil, Perú) to cold (southern Chile). Overall, the infrastructure is weaker than that of Spain, and only the beaches of oceanfront hotels provide European-level accommodations. On the other hand, if you are the adventurous type, Latin America offers what few other lands can: miles of uncluttered open space.

Swimming

Excuse me please, is there a ... here?
Perdone, por favor, ¿hay aquí...

swimming pool
una piscina?

outdoor pool
una piscina al aire libre?

indoor pool
una piscina cubierta?

One ticket, please.
Por favor, una entrada (*Am* un boleto).

Can you tell me where the ... are?
¿Me podría decir dónde están...

showers
las duchas?

changing rooms
los vestidores?

Is the beach …
La playa,

sandy?
¿es de arena?

rocky?
¿es pedregosa?

Are there sea urchins/jellyfish?
¿Hay aquí erizos de mar/medusas?

Is there a strong current?
¿Es fuerte la corriente?

Is it dangerous for children?
¿Es peligroso para los niños?

When is the low tide/high tide?
¿A qué hora es la marea baja/alta?

I would like to rent…
Quisiera alquilar …

a deck chair
una tumbona

a beach umbrella
una sombrilla

a boat
un bote

a pair of water skis
unos esquís acuáticos

How much is it per hour/per day?
¿Cuánto cuesta esto por hora / por día?

Air mattress	el colchón de aire
Beach volleyball	el voley playa
Fins	las aletas (de natación)
Jet bike	la moto de agua
Kiddy pool	piscina infantil
Lifeguard	vigilante (de piscina)
Non-swimmers	no nadadores
Nudist beach	playa nudista
Paddle boat	barca de pedales
Sunbathing area	el lugar para asolearse
Swim, to	nadar
Swimmer	el nadador
Water ski	el esquí acuático
Water ski, to	practicar el esquí acuático
Water wings	los flotadores (de brazos)
Windscreen	biombo

Other Activities and Sports

What athletic activities/facilities are there here?
¿Qué posibilidades hay aquí de hacer deporte?

Is there … here?
¿Hay aquí…

a golf course
un campo de golf?

a tennis court
una pista (*Am* cancha) de tenis?

Where can I … around here?
¿Dónde se puede aquí…

fish with a rod
pescar con caña?

go on an excursion
hacer excursiones?

Where can I rent…?
¿Dónde puedo tomar prestado…?

I would like to do a … course for beginners/take an advanced … course.
Me gustaría hacer un curso de… de principiantes/avanzados.

Water Sports

Boat excursion	la excursión en bote
Boating certificate	el carnet náutico
Canoe	canoa
Canyoning	descenso de barrancos
Houseboat	la embarcación habitable
Paddleboat	barca de pedales
Pedal, to	pedalear
Pickup service	servicio de recogida
Power boat	lancha motora
Rafting	el rafting, descenso de aguas bravas
Regatta	regata
Row, to	remar
Rowboat	barca de remos
Rower	remero
Rubber boat	el bote neumático
Sail, to	navegar (a vela)
Sailboat	velero
Sailing excursion	la excursión en velero
Speedboat	la lancha de carrera
Surf, to	practicar el surf
Surfboard	plancha/tabla de surf
Wind conditions	vientos, estado de los
Windsurf, to	practicar el windsurf

Diving

Air bottle	tanque de aire comprimido
Dive, to	bucear
Diving equipment	equipo de buceo
Diving mask	las gafas de buceo
Harpoon	el arpón submarino
Snorkel	tubo de buceo
Snorkel, to	nadar con tubo de buceo
Wet suit	el traje isotérmico/de neopreno

Fishing

Deep-sea fishing	pesca marítima/de altura
Fishing license	licencia de pesca
Fishing rod	caña de pescar
Fishing with a rod	pescar con caña
Harbor master's office	la dirección del puerto
Off-season	veda

Ball Games

Ball	pelota, el balón
Baseball	el baloncesto
Goal	portería
Goalie	portero
Half time	medio tiempo
Handball	balonmano
Net	la red
Rugby	el rugby
Soccer	el fútbol
Soccer field	campo (*Am* cancha) de fútbol
Soccer match	partido de fútbol
Team	equipo
Volleyball	el voleibol

Tennis/Badminton/Squash

Badminton	el bádminton
Doubles	el doble
Flood lights	la iluminación
Paddle	paleta
Racquet	raqueta
Shuttlecock	el volante de badminton
Singles	(partido) individual
Squash	el squash
Table tennis	el ping-pong, el tenis de mesa
Tennis	el tenis
Tennis racquet	raqueta (de tenis)

ACTIVE VACATIONS

123

Physical Fitness and Weight Training

aerobics	(el) aerobic
bodybuilding	ejercicios de desarrollo muscular
fitness training	la preparación física
gym equipment	equipo de gimnasia
health club	centro de gimnasia
jogging	footing
run, to	correr
spinal column physiotherapy	fisioterapia para la columna vertebral
stretching	estiramiento

Wellness

Massage	el masaje
Pool	piscina
Sauna	sauna
Solarium	solario
Turkish bath	baño de vapor

Biking

Bicycle	bicicleta
Bike helmet	casco de bicicleta
Bike path	pista para bicicletas
Bike pump	bomba de aire
Cycling	ciclismo
Cycling tour	la excursión en bici(cleta)
Inner tube	cámara
Mountain bike	bicicleta de montaña, el mountain bike
Racing bike	bicicleta de carreras
Ride a bike, to	montar (*Am* andar) en bicicleta
Spoke	radio
Tire	neumático
Tire repair kit	equipo para reparar neumáticos
Trekking	el trekking

Hiking and Mountain Climbing

I would like to go on an excursion in the mountains.
Quisiera hacer una excursión por las montañas.

Can you show me an interesting route on the map?
¿Puede usted indicarme en el mapa un itinerario interesante?

Backpack	mochila
Climbing boots	botas de alpinismo
Day trip	la excursión de un día

124

Free climbing	escalada libre
Hike, to	hacer excursiones
Hiking	excursionismo, senderismo
Hiking path	sendero (para excursiones a pie)
Map	el mapa
Mountain guide	el guía de montaña
Mountain shelter	refugio de montaña
Peak	pico
Rescue service	servicio de salvamento
Rock-climbing	escalar
Route	ruta
Safety rope	soga de seguridad
Trekking	el trekking

Horseback Riding

Horse	caballo
Polo	polo
Ride	paseo a caballo
Ride, to	montar a caballo
Riding school	escuela de equitación
Saddle	montura

Golf

Clubhouse	casa club
Eighteen-hole course	campo de dieciocho hoyos
Golf	el golf
Golf ball	pelota de golf
Golf club	el club de golf
Golfer	jugador de golf
Greenfee	cuota de admisión
Handicap	handicap
Links	campo de golf
Tee-off	punto de salida

Gliding

Glider	el planeador
Gliding	vuelo sin motor
Hang gliding	vuelo libre, ala delta
Hot-air balloon	globo aerostático
Parachuting	paracaidismo
Paragliding	el parapente
Take-off area	punto de salida
Thermals	la térmica
Ultralight	ultraligero

ACTIVE VACATIONS

125

One chairlift ticket, please.
Un boleto de telesilla, por favor.

When is he last trip up/down the hill?
¿A qué hora es la última subida/bajada?

Alpine skiing	el esquí alpino
Cable railway	el funicular, teleférico
Chairlift	el telesilla
Cross-country skiing	el esquí de fondo
Curling	el curling
Day pass	el forfait (*Am* boleto) válido para un día
Ice hockey	el hockey sobre hielo
Ice skates	los patines de hielo
Ice-skate, to	patinar sobre hielo
Ice-skating	el patinaje sobre hielo
Ice-skating rink	pista de hielo
Powder snow	la nieve polvo
Ski	el esquí
Ski binding	la fijación (de los esquís)
Ski boots	las botas para esquiar
Ski goggles	las gafas de esquí
Ski instructor	el profesor de esquí
Ski poles	los bastones de esquí
Ski, to	esquiar
Skiing lesson	curso de esquí
Sled	trineo
Sledding, to go	montar en trineo
Snowboard	el snowboard
Snowmobile	snowmobile
Snowrafting	el snowrafting
Summit station	la estación de esquí
Tow lift	el telearrastre
Track	trazado
Valley station	la estación inferior
Weekly pass	abono semanal

Archery	tiro al arco
Bocce	juego de bochas
Bowling	juego de bolos
Bungee jumping	el puenting
Inline skater	el patinador (de patines en línea)
Inline skates	los patines en línea
Rafting	descenso de aguas bravas, el rafting
Roller skates	los patines de ruedas

126

Roller-skate, to	patinar
Skateboard	el monopatín
Skateboarding, to go	patinar con monopatín
Track and field	atletismo

Sporting Events

What sporting events are there here?
¿Qué actos deportivos hay aquí?

I would like to watch a soccer game.
Quisiera ver el partido de fútbol.

When/Where is it?
¿Cuándo/Dónde es?

How much is the ticket?
¿Cuánto cuesta la entrada (*Am* el boleto)?

What's the score?
¿A cuánto están?

Two to one; one to one.
Dos a uno; uno a uno.

Foul!
Falta.

Nice shot!
¡Buen disparo!

Goal!
¡Gol!

Athlete	el/la deportista
Athletic field	campo (*Am* cancha) de deportes
Center, to	centrar
Championship	campeonato
Competition	la competición
Cycle racing	carrera ciclista
Defeat	derrota
Free kick	el golpe franco
Lose, to	perder
Match	juego, partido
Offside	fuera de juego
Overtime	sobretiempo
Pass	el pase
Penalty	sanción
Program	el programa
Race	carrera
Referee	árbitro
Stadium	estadio
Ticket	entrada, el billete (*Am* boleto)

Ticket office	caja
Tie	empate
Win	victoria
Win, to	ganar

Creative Vacations

I would like to attend a...
Me gustaría asistir a un...

pottery course.
un curso de cerámica.

Spanish course.
un curso de español.

for beginners.
para principiantes.

for advanced learners.
de nivel avanzado.

Do you need previous knowledge?
¿Se necesitan conocimientos previos?

When is the registration deadline?
¿Hasta cuándo dura el período de inscripción?

Are the costs of materials included?
¿Se incluyen los gastos de material?

What should I bring along?
¿Qué se necesita traer?

Belly dancing	la danza del vientre
Carpentry workshop	el taller de carpintería
Cooking	cocina
Course	curso
Dance theater	teatro bailado
Drama workshop	taller de teatro
Language course	curso de lenguaje
Nude	desnudo
Oil painting	pintura al óleo
Paint, to	pintar
Photography	fotografía
Sew, to	coser, hacer costura
Silk painting	pintura sobre seda
Theater ensemble	grupo de teatro
Watercolor painting	pintar con acuarela
Working with gold	labrar orfebrería
Workshop	el taller
Yoga	el yoga

Entertainment

Festivals

In the summer, Spanish theaters close and movie theaters don't show any new films. On the other hand, city blocks, neighborhoods, villages, and towns all over Spain hold festivals. You should expect to find culinary delights, dancing, and music until the wee hours at these events. In addition, summer is the time of the big outdoor concerts and the theater and film festivals. But you can enjoy cultural events free of charge in the other months as well: classical concerts, exhibitions, lectures, and the like. For details, see the local section of the newspaper or ask at the tourist information office.

Theater—Concert—Movies

Could you tell me what's playing at the theater tonight?
¿Me podría decir qué hay esta noche en el teatro?

What's on at the movies tomorrow evening?
¿Qué hay mañana por la tarde en el cine?

Are there concerts in the cathedral?
¿Hay conciertos en la catedral?

Can you recommend a good play?
¿Puede usted recomendarme una buena obra de teatro?

When does the performance start?
¿A qué hora comienza la representación?

Where can I get tickets?
¿Dónde se pueden adquirir los billetes (*Am* boletos)?

Two tickets for tonight, please.
Dos entradas (*Am* boletos) para esta noche, por favor.

Two tickets for ..., please.
Dos entradas para..., por favor.

May I have a program?
¿Me puede dar un programa?

Advance ticket sales	venta anticipada
Coat check	el guardarropa
Festival	el festival
Interval	entreacto, descanso
Presentation	presentación
Program	el programa
Ticket	entrada, el billete
Ticket office	caja

Theater

Act	acto
Actor/actress	actor/actriz
Ballet	el ballet
Box	palco
Cabaret	el cabaré
Comedian	cómico
Comedy	comedia
Dancer	bailarín/bailarina
Director	director
Drama	el drama
First/second row	primera/segunda fila
Music hall	teatro de variedades
Musical	comedia musical, el musical
Open-air theater	teatro al aire libre
Opera	ópera
Operetta	zarzuela
Orchestra	platea
Performance	espectáculo, la representación
Play	espectáculo; obra de teatro
Premiere	estreno
Production	la escenificación
Program	el programa
Tragedy	tragedia

Concert

Blues	el blues
Choir	coro
Classical music	música clásica
Composer	compositor/compositora
Concert	concierto
Concert of chamber music	concierto de cámara
Concert of sacred music	concierto de música sacra, concierto en la iglesia
Symphony concert	concierto sinfónico
Conductor	director/directora (de orquesta)
Folk	folk
Folk music	música folclórica
Jazz	el jazz
Orchestra	orquesta
Pop	el pop
Rap	el rap
Reggae	el reggae
Rock	rock
Singer	el/la cantante

Soloist	el/la solista
Soul	el soul
Techno	el tecno

Movies

Directed by	la dirección
Film	película, el film(e)
Action movie	película de acción
Animated movie	película de dibujos animados
Black and white movie	película en blanco y negro
Classic	un clásico del cine
Comedy	comedia
Documentary	el documental
Drama	drama
Science fiction movie	película de ciencia ficción
Short film	el cortometraje
Thriller	película de terror, thriller
Western	el western, la película del oeste
Movie actor/actress	el actor/la actriz de cine
Leading role	el papel principal
Movie theater	el cine
Drive-in movie	el cine al aire libre
Screen	pantalla
Original version	versión original
Special effects	los efectos especiales
Subtitles	subtítulo

Nightlife

In Spain, nightlife begins very late—often not until midnight—and can last until morning.

First, people eat in a restaurant with friends. Next they go somewhere for a drink, and finally they go to discos or festival halls.

Anyone who still hasn't had enough can top it all off with chocolate and *churros* for breakfast.

What's there to do around here at night?
¿Qué se puede hacer en este lugar por las noches?

Is there a good/cozy bar here?
¿Hay por aquí un bar/una taberna acogedor/a?

Don't you have a disco close by?
¿No hay ninguna discoteca por aquí?

132

Where can you go dancing here?
¿Dónde se puede ir a bailar por aquí?

Could I have this dance (one more time)?
¿Bailamos (otra vez)?

Band	banda, conjunto
Bar	el bar
Bingo *(game of chance,* . . .	bingo
a kind of lottery, often	
played in Spain)	
Casino	casino
Concert	concierto
Dance band	orquesta de baile
Dance, to	bailar
Disco	discoteca
Folk concert	espectáculo folclórico
Folklore	el folclore
Gambling	juego de azar
Go out, to	salir
Live music	música en directo
Nightclub	el club nocturno
Show	espectáculo
Tavern	el bar, la taberna, la tasca

Festivals and Events

Public festivals and special events

Madrid:	*Fiestas de San Isidro* (mid-May)
	Numerous cultural offerings, especially bullfights in the arena
Barcelona:	*Festes de la Mercé* (late September)
	Parade with music, giants, and fire-spewing dragons; also many outdoor concerts
Pamplona:	*San Fermín* (July)
	Bulls run in the streets, with the men of Pamplona, dressed all in white with a red scarf, running ahead of the bulls
Seville:	*Semana Santa* (Holy Week)
	Impressive procession
Valencia:	*Fallas* (March 19th)
	Large papier-mâché figures are burned.

Could you tell me when is the ... festival?
¿Me podría decir cuándo es... el festival de...?

from...to...
del... al...

in August each year
cada año en agosto

every other year
bienal

What is it, exactly?
¿De qué se trata exactamente?

Can any take part?
¿Puede participar cualquiera?

All-Spain bike race	Vuelta Ciclista a España
Main state holiday	fiesta mayor
Bullfight	la corrida de toros
Circus	circo
Parade; cavalcade (to honor .	el desfile; cabalgata
the Three Wise Men)	(cabalgata de Reyes)
Procession (Holy Week's) ..	la procesión (de Semana Santa)
Vervain (night festival on ..	verbena (San Juan; San Pedro)
the eve of a saint's day,	
e.g., St. John, Saint Peter)	

Shopping

Strolling around town

Spain is no longer as inexpensive as it used to be. Nonetheless, you can eat and drink relatively economically. But for good and inexpensive food, Latin America is the place to be: phenomenal steaks in Argentina, exquisite fish in Chile, wonderful native meals in Peru, every country has magnificent dishes at a price everybody can afford.

Both in Spain and Latin America, it is also worth seeking out little artisans' workshops that produce fabric, furniture, or decorative products made of ceramics. Although connoisseurs complain that uniqueness and spontaneity are fast disappearing in the arts and crafts world, quality has greatly improved.

Questions

I'm looking for ...

Are you being helped?
¿Ya le/la atienden?

Thank you, I'm just looking around.
Gracias, sólo quiero mirar un poco.

I would like...
Quisiera... / Desearía... / Me gustaría...

Do you have...?
¿Tiene usted...?

Can I get you anything else?
¿Desea alguna cosa más?

Bargaining and Buying

Haggling is not customary in Spain, even though it is still occasionally practiced at flea markets.

How much is it?
¿Cuánto cuesta?

That's expensive!
¡Qué caro que es!

I could only afford to pay...
Como mucho puedo pagar...

I will take it.
Bien, me lo llevo.

Do you take credit cards?
¿Aceptan ustedes tarjetas de crédito?

Stores

Excuse me, please, where can I get...?
Perdone, por favor, ¿dónde hay...?

Daily hours
horario de apertura

abierto	Open
cerrado	Closed
cerrado por vacaciones	Closed for vacations

Antique shop	tienda de antigüedades
Art dealer	(el/la comerciante de) objetos de arte
Bakery	panadería; pastelería, confitería
Barber shop	peluquería
Beauty parlor	salón de belleza
Bookstore	librería
Boutique	la boutique
Butcher shop	carnicería
Candy store	confitería, pastelería
Delicatessen	(tienda de) comestibles, especialidades (*Am* fiambrería)
Department store	los grandes almacenes
Drugstore	droguería
Dry cleaners	tintorería, limpieza en seco
Electrical appliances store . .	(tienda de) artículos eléctricos
Flea market	rastro
Flower shop	floristería
Fruit and vegetable stand . .	frutería y verdulería
Gift shop	tienda de recuerdos, souvenirs
Grocery store	tienda de comestibles (*Am* el almacén)
Hardware store	ferretería
Health food store	tienda de productos naturistas y dietéticos
Jewelry store	joyería

Kiosk	quiosco
Laundromat	lavandería
Leather goods store	(tienda de) artículos de piel/cuero
Liquor store	tienda de vinos y licores
Macrobiotics store	tienda macrobiótica
Market	mercado
Newspaper stand	el vendedor de periódicos
Optician's	óptica
Perfume store	perfumería
Pharmacy	farmacia
Photo store	(tienda de) artículos fotográficos
Seafood store	pescadería
Second-hand store	prendero, trapero
Shoe store	zapatería
Shoemaker	zapatero
Sporting goods store	tienda de artículos deportivos
Stationery store	papelería
Supermarket	supermercado
Taylor/dressmaker	el sastre/la modista
Tobacco store	estanco (*Am* cigarrería)
Toy store	juguetería, tienda de juguetes
Travel agency	agencia de viajes
Watchmaker's	relojero
Wine store	el almacén de vinos

Books, Magazines, and Stationery

The sensationalist newspapers are very popular everywhere. Almost everybody is interested in reading about the life of the rich and powerful, without taking their fates all too seriously. The Spanish royal family, however, is approached with love and respect.

I would like...
Quisiera...

a newspaper in English.
un periódico en inglés.

a magazine.
una revista.

a tourist guide.
una guía turística.

a map of this area.
un mapa de esta zona.

Books, Magazines, and Newspapers

Book	libro
City map	plano de la ciudad
Comic book	comic, tebeo
Cookbook	libro de cocina
Hard cover book	libro de tapa gruesa
Magazine	revista
Map	el mapa
Newspaper	periódico
Novel	novela
Paperback	libro de bolsillo
Road map	el mapa de carreteras
Romance novel	novela romántica
Science-fiction book	novela de ciencia ficción
Thriller	novela policíaca
Travel guide	guía turística
Women's magazine	revista para mujeres

Stationery

Ball point pen	bolígrafo (*Am* lapicero de bolilla)
Color pencil	el lapiz de color
Coloring book	cuaderno de colorear
Envelope	el sobre
Glue	la goma, el pegamento
Notebook	cuaderno
Notepad	la libreta
Paper	el papel
Pencil	el lápiz
Postcard	la postal
Stationery	el papel de escribir

CDs and Cassettes

> also Electrical Goods and Concert

Do you have any of ... CDs/cassettes?
¿Tiene usted discos compactos/casetes de ...?

I would like to buy a CD with typical Spanish music.
Me gustaría comprar un CD con música típica española.

May I listen to a sample right here?
¿Puedo escucharlo un poco aquí mismo?

Cassette	la/el casete
CD (compact disc)	el CD (disco compacto)
CD player	el tocadiscos
DVD	el DVD (deh-veh-deh)
Headphones	los auriculares
MP3 receiver	el receptor de MP3
	(ehmeh-peh-trehs)
Speaker	el altavoz (*Am* el altoparlante)
Walkman®	el walkman®

Drugstore Items

Band-aid®	tirita
Brush	cepillo
Chapstick®	crema de labios
Comb	el peine
Cosmetics	cosméticos
Cotton	el algodón
Cotton swabs	bastoncillo de algodón
Cream	crema
Dental floss	seda dental
Deodorant	el desodorante
Detergent	el detergente
Dishwashing liquid	el lavavajillas
Disposable shaver	rastrillo desechable
Hair band	cinta para el pelo
Hair gel	el gel para el pelo
Hair-removing cream	crema depiladora
Hairpins	las horquillas
Hand cream	crema hidratante para las manos
Lipstick	el pintalabios
Lotion	la loción
Mascara	el rímel
Mirror	espejo
Moisturizing cream	crema hidratante
Mouthwash	enjuague bucal
Nail polish	laca de uñas
Nail scissors	tijera de uñas
Nail-polish remover	el quitaesmaltes
Night cream	crema de noche
Panty liners	el salva-slip
Paper tissues	los pañuelos de papel

Perfume	el perfume
Prophylactic	preservativo
Razor blade	hoja de afeitar
Sanitary napkin	toalla higiénica
Setting gel	gel fijador
Setting lotion	el fijador (para el pelo)
Shampoo	el champú
Shaver	maquinilla de afeitar
Shaving brush	brocha de afeitar
Shaving cream	espuma de afeitar
Shower gel	el gel de ducha
Soap	el jabón
SPF	(el) factor de protección solar
Suntan lotion	la loción solar
Tampons	los tampones
mini/normal/super/	mini/normal/súper/
super plus	súper plus
Toilet paper	el papel higiénico
Toothbrush	cepillo de dientes
Toothpaste	pasta de dientes
Toothpick	mondadientes
Tweezers	las pinzas
Washcloth	paño para frotar
Washing-up brush	cepillo de espalda

Electrical Goods

➢ **also Photo Supplies and CDs and Cassettes**

Adapter	el adaptador
Alarm clock	el despertador
Battery	batería
Battery charger	el recargador (para pilas)
Bulb	bombilla
Extension cord	el cordón de empalme
Hairdryer	el secador de pelo
Laptop	la computadora portátil
Organizer	agenda electrónica
Plug	clavija de enchufe
Pocket calculator	calculadora de bolsillo

Photo Supplies

➢ also Filming and Photographing

I would like...
Quisiera... / Desearía... / Me gustaría...

a roll of film for this camera.
un carrete para esta cámara.

color (slide) film
una película en color (para diapositivas).

a roll for 36 shots.
un carrete de 36 fotografías.

...doesn't work.
... no funciona.

It's broken. Can you fix it?
Está estropeado. ¿Podrían arreglármelo?

Black-and-white film	película en blanco y negro
Camcorder	la camcórder
Digital camera	cámara fotográfica digital
DVD	DVD
Film speed	la sensibilidad de la película
Flash	el flash
Instant camera	cámara fotográfica instantánea
Lens	la lente
Light meter	fotómetro
Megapixel	el megapixel
Self-timer	el disparador automático
Shutter	el disparador
Telephoto lens	teleobjetivo
Tripod	el trípode
Underwater camera	cámara fotográfica sumergible
Videocamera	cámara de vídeo, filmadora
Videocassette	la videocinta
Videofilm	película de vídeo
Videorecorder	la videograbadora
Viewfinder	el visor

Hairdresser/Barber

Shampoo and blow dry, please.
Lavar y secar, por favor.

Wash and cut/Dry cut, please.
Lavar y cortar/Corte sin lavar, por favor.

I would like...
Quisiera... / Desearía...

Just trim the ends.
Recorte sólo las puntas.

Not too short/Really short/A bit shorter, please.
No demasiado corto / Muy corto / Un poco más corto, por favor.

My ears should be showing/should not be showing.
Que no me tape / Que me cubra las orejas.

A shave, please.
Afeitar, por favor.

Just a trim. / Fix the beard, please.
Córteme un poco/Arrégleme la barba, por favor.

Thank you. That's fine.
Muchas gracias. Está muy bien así.

Bangs	flequillo
Beard	barba
Blond	rubio
Blow-dry, to	secar
Comb, to	peinar
Curlers	rulo (*Am* rulero)
Curls	los rizos (*Am* los rulos)
Dandruff	caspa
Do someone's hair, to	peinar
Dye, to	teñir
Hair	pelo
dry hair	pelo seco
greasy hair	pelo graso
Hairstyle	peinado
Highlights	las mechas
Layered out	escalado
Mustache	el bigote
Part	raya
Perm	la permanente
Put in a rinse, to	dar reflejos
Set	peinado
Shampoo	el champú
Sideburns	las patillas
Wig	peluca

Household Goods

Aluminum foil	el papel de aluminio
Bottle opener	el abridor
Can opener	el abrelatas
Candles	las velas
Charcoal	el carbón para la barbacoa
Clothesline	cuerda de la ropa
Clothespins	las pinzas de la ropa
Cooler	la nevera portátil
Corkscrew	el sacacorchos
Cup	taza
Fork	el tenedor
Freezer pack	bolsita de hielo
Garbage bag	bolsa de la basura
Glass	vaso de vidrio
Grill	parrilla, barbacoa
Knife	cuchillo
Lighter	el encendedor
Methyl alcohol	el alcohol (para quemar)
Paper napkin	las servilletas de papel
Plastic bag	bolsa de plástico
Plastic cup	vaso de plástico
Plastic wrap	plástico para conservación de alimentos
Pocket knife	navaja
Spoon	cuchara
Thermos®	termo

Groceries

What can I do for you?
¿Qué desea?

I would like...
Déme..., por favor.

  a kilo of...
  un kilo de...

  ten slices of...
  diez tajadas de...

  a piece of...
  un trozo de...

  a package of...
  un paquete de...

  a jar of...
  un frasco de...

a can of...
una lata de...

a bottle of...
una botella de...

a bag
una bolsa

May I add a bit more?
¿Puedo ponerle un poquito más?

May I try a bit of this?
¿Me permite probar un poco de esto?

That's it, thank you.
Eso es todo, gracias.

Fruit	**Fruta**
Apples	las manzanas
Apricots	los albaricoques
Avocado	el aguacate
Banana	plátano
Blackberries	las moras
Cherries	las cerezas
Chestnuts	las castañas
Coconut	coco
Dates	los dátiles
Figs	los higos
Fruit	fruta
Grapefruit	pomelo
Grapes	las uvas
Lemons	los limones
Medlars	los nísperos
Melon	el melón
Olives	las aceitunas
Oranges	las naranjas
Peaches	los melocotones
Pears	las peras
Pineapple	piña (*Am* el ananás)
Plums	las ciruelas
Pomegranates	granada
Strawberries	las fresas, los fresones (*Am* la frutilla)
Tangerines	las mandarinas
Watermelon	sandía

146

Vegetables	Verdura
Artichokes	las alcachofas
Asparagus	el espárrago
Beans	las judías (*Am* los porotos, los frijoles)
green beans	las judías verdes (*Am* las chauchas)
haricot beans	las judías blancas
Bird pepper	guindilla
Cabbage	repollo, berza, la col
Carrots	las zanahorias
Cauliflower	la coliflor
Celery	apio
Chards	las acelgas
Chickpeas	los garbanzos
Chicory	endibia
Corn	el maíz
Cucumber	pepino
Eggplants	las berenjenas
Garlic	ajo
Leek	puerro
Lentils	las lentejas
Lettuce	lechuga
Onions	las cebollas
Parsley	el perejil
Peas	los guisantes (*Am* las arvejas, las alverjas)
Pepper	pimiento
Potatoes	las patatas
Pumpkin	calabaza
Spinach	las espinacas
Sweet potatoes	boniatos
Tomatoes	los tomates
Vegetables	las verduras; las legumbres
Zucchini	el calabacín

Bread and Sweets	Pastelería, dulces...
Bread	el pan
white bread	el pan blanco
whole wheat bread	el pan de centeno
Buns	panecillo
sandwich	bocadillo (*Am* el sándwich)
Cake	tarta, el pastel

Candy	los caramelos; los dulces, las golosinas
Cereals	los cereales
Chocoate bar	barra/barrita de chocolate
Chocolate	el chocolate
Cookies	las galletas dulces
Crackers	las galletas saladas
Ice cream	helado
Marmalade	mermelada
Rolled oats	los copos de avena
Toast	tostada

Eggs and Dairy Products — Huevos y productos lácteos

Baked custard	el flan
Butter	mantequilla (*Am* manteca)
Cheese	queso
Cottage cheese	el requesón
Cream	nata
sour cream	nata agria
whipped cream	nata batida/montada
Cream custard	las natillas
Eggs	los huevos
Milk	la leche
skimmed milk	la leche semidesnatada
Yogurt	el yogur

Meats and Cold Cuts — Carnes y embutidos

Beef	la carne de vaca
Chicken	pollo
Cold cuts	el embutido, los fiambres variados
Ground meat	la carne picada
Ham	el jamón
cooked ham	el jamón de york, el jamón cocido
dry ham	el jamón seco
Kid's meat	cabrito
Lamb	la carne de cordero
Liver pate	el paté de hígado
Liverwurst	embutido de hígado
Meat	la carne

Mutton	la carne de carnero
Pork	la carne de cerdo
Rabbit	conejo
Rib	costilla
Salami	el salami, el salchichón
Sausage meats	embutido
Sausages	salchicha
Snails	los caracoles
Stew	estofado (a la húngara)
Veal	la carne de ternera

Fish and Meats — Pescados y mariscos

Angler	el rape
Calamari	los calamares, los chipirones, la sepia
Clams	las almejas
Crab	cangrejo, jaiba
Eel	anguila
Fish	pescado
Gilthead, dorado	dorada
Herring	el arenque
Mackerel	caballa
Mussels	los mejillones
Oysters	las ostras
Perch	perca
Shrimp	las gambas, los camarones
Sole	lenguado
Swordfish	el pez espada
Tuna	bonito, el atún

Spices — Expecias

Aniseed	semilla de anís
Basil	albahaca
Bay leaves	el laurel
Bird pepper	guindilla verde
Borage	borraja
Chervil	perifollo
Chili	chile
Chives	cebollino
Cinnamon	canela
Cloves	clavo
Coriander	cilantro
Cumin	comino

Dill	eneldo
Garlic	ajo
Ginger	jengibre
Herbs	las hierbas
Marjoram	mejorana
Mint	menta
Nutmeg	la nuez moscada
Onion	cebolla
Oregano	orégano
Paprika	pimiento
Parsley	perejil
Pepper	pimienta
Rosemary	romero
Saffron	el azafrán
Sage	salvia
Savory	ajedrea
Thyme	tomillo

This and That — Otros

Almonds	las almendras
Bouillon cube	caldo en cubito
Butter	mantequilla (*Am* manteca)
Dry fruit	los frutos secos
Flour	harina
Honey	la miel
Ketchup	ketchup
Margarine	margarina
Mayonnaise	mayonesa, mahonesa
Mustard	mostaza
Oil	el aceite
Olive oil	el aceite de oliva
Rice	el arroz
Salt	la sal
Spaghetti	los espaguetis
Sugar	el azúcar
Vinegar	el vinagre

Drinks — Bebidas

Apple juice	zumo de manzana
Beer	cerveza
nonalcoholic beer	cerveza sin alcohol

Champagne	el cava, el champán
Coffee	el café
decaffeinated coffee	café descafeinado
Lemonade	limonada
Mineral water	(el) agua mineral
with/without gas	con / sin gas
Orange juice	zumo de naranja
Tea	el té
black tea	té negro
chamomile tea	la infusión manzanilla
fruit tea	infusión de frutas
green tea	té verde
herbal tea	tisana
peppermint tea	la infusión de menta
rose hip tea	infusión de escaramujo
Teabag	bolsita de té
Wine	vino
red wine	vino tinto
rosé wine	vino rosado
white wine	vino blanco

Fashion

> also Colors

Clothing

Can you show me ... please?
¿Podría enseñarme..., por favor?

May I try it on?
¿Puedo probármelo/la?

What size do you take?
¿Qué talla tiene usted?

It's too...
Me resulta demasiado...

tight/loose
estrecho (*Am* angosto)/ancho.

short/long.
corto/largo.

small/large.
pequeño/grande.

It's a good fit. I'll take it.
Me va muy bien. Me lo quedo.

It's not exactly what I had in mind.
No es exactamente lo que yo quería.

Bathing cap	gorro de baño
Bathrobe	el albornoz
Belt	cinturón
Bikini	el biquini
Blazer	el blazer
Blouse	blusa
Bow tie	pajarita
Bra	el sujetador, el sostén (*Am* el brasier)
Briefs	el calzoncillo, los calzoncillos
Cap	gorra
Cardigan	chaqueta de punto, rebeca (*Am* saco tejido)
Coat	abrigo
Cotton	el algodón
Dress	vestido
Gloves	los guantes
Hat	sombrero
sunhat	sombrero
Jacket	chaqueta (*Am* saco)
Jeans	los tejanos, los vaqueros
Jogging suit	el chándal
Leather	cuero
Leotards	los leotardos
Linen	lino
Nylon	nilón
Pajama	el pijama
Pants	el pantalón
Panty	braga;
Parka	el anorak
Pullover	el jersey (*Am* el pulóver)
Raincoat	el impermeable
Scarf	pañuelo de cuello
Shirt	camisa
Shorts	el pantalón corto
Silk	seda
Silk panties	los pantys de seda
Silk stockings	las medias de seda
Ski pants	el pantalón de esquí
Skirt	falda
Sleeve	manga
Socks	los calcetines

Stockings	las medias
Suit	el traje
Sweat pants	el pantalón de deporte
Swimming trunks	el traje de baño
Swimsuit	el traje de baño, bañador
T-Shirt	camiseta
Tie	corbata
Tights	las mallas
Umbrella	el paraguas
Undershirt	camiseta
Underwear	ropa interior
Vest	chaleco
Wool	lana

Cleaning

I would like to have these things dry-cleaned/washed, please.
Quisiera que me limpiaran en seco/que me lavaran esta ropa.

When will they be ready.
¿Cuándo estarán listas?

| dry-clean, to | limpiar en seco |
| iron, to | planchar |

Optician

Would you please fix these glasses for me?
¿Puede usted arreglarme estas gafas (*Am* estos anteojos/lentes) por favor?

I am near-sighted/far-sighted.
Soy miope/présbita.

What is your eye prescription?
¿Cuál es su capacidad visual?

to the right..., to the left...
a la derecha..., a la izquierda...

When can I pick up my glasses?
¿Cuándo puedo recoger las gafas?

I would like...
Necesito...

    contact lens solution.
    líquido para conservar lentillas.

cleaning solution.
líquido limpiador.

for hard/soft contact lenses.
para lentes de contacto duras/blandas.

some sunglasses.
unas gafas de sol.

a pair of binoculars.
unos prismáticos.

Shoes and Leather Goods

I want a pair of ... shoes.
Quiero un par de zapatos...

I take a size ...
Calzo el número...

They are a bit too tight.
Me aprietan un poco.

They are too big.
Son demasiado grandes.

Attaché case	maletín
Backpack	mochila
Bag	bolsa de viaje
Belt	el cinturón
Boots	las botas
Duffel bag	talego de lona
Fanny pack	la riñonera
Leather coat	abrigo de cuero
Leather jacket	chaqueta de cuero
Leather pants	el pantalón de cuero
Purse	cartera, bolsa (de mano)
Rubber boots	las botas de goma
Sandals	las sandalias
Shoe	zapato
Shoe brush	cepillo del calzado
Shoe polish	el betún
Shoelaces	los cordones
Shoulder bag	(bolsa en) bandolera
Shoulder strap	la bandolera
Ski boots	las botas de esquí
Slippers	las chancletas, las chanclas
Sole	suela
Suitcase	maleta
Tennis shoes	las zapatillas de deporte
Wheeled tote bag	maleta/maletín con ruedas

Souvenirs

I would like...
Quisiera...

a nice souvenir.
un recuerdo bonito.

something typical of this area.
algo típico de esta zona.

About how much are you thinking of spending?
¿Cuánto quiere usted gastar aproximadamente?

I would like something that is not too expensive.
Quisiera algo que no sea demasiado caro.

That's pretty.
Esto es muy bonito.

Thank you, but I couldn't see anything I like.
Gracias, pero no veo nada que me guste.

Ceramics	cerámica
Folk art store	tienda de productos folclóricos
Genuine	auténtico
Handmade	hecho a mano
Jewelry	las joyas
Pottery	los objetos de cerámica
Regional/Typical products . .	productos regionales/típicos
Souvenir	recuerdo
Textiles	los tejidos
Woodcarving	tallas de madera

Tobacco

A pack/A carton of cigarettes, please.
Un paquete/Un cartón de cigarrillos, por favor.

filter-tipped/without filter, please.
con/sin filtro, por favor.

Give me ten cigars/cigarillos, please.
Déme diez puros (*Am* cigarros)/puritos (*Am* cigarros pequeños), por favor.

A pack of pipe tobacco, please.
Un paquete de tabaco de pipa, por favor.

Ashtray	cenicero
Cigar	puro
Cigarette	cigarrillo, pitillo, cigarro

Cigarillo	purito
Lighter	encendedor
Match	cerilla
Pipe	pipa

Watches and Jewelry

Bracelet	pulsera, el brazalete
Costume jewelry	bisutería
Crystal	el cristal (de roca)
Earrings	los pendientes (*Am* los aretes)
Gold	oro
Jewelry	las joyas
Necklace	el collar, cadena
Pearl	perla
Pendant	el colgante
Pin	el broche
Ring	anillo
Silver	plata
Stud earring	pendiente de botón
Tiepin	alfiler de corbata
Travel alarm	despertador de viaje
Water-resistant watch	reloj resistente al agua
Wristwatch	el reloj de pulsera
ladies'/men's	para señoras / caballeros

OL.
AMOMILL

MENTHOL.
ERIAN.

OL.
AURANT.
FLOR.

Health

At the Pharmacy

Where is the nearest pharmacy (with 24-hour service), please?
¿Dónde está la farmacia (de guardia) más cercana, por favor?

Can you give me something for ..., please?
¿Me puede dar algo para..., por favor?

You need a prescription for this.
Sólo con receta médica.

➢ **also At the Doctor's Office**

Aspirin	aspirina
Band-aid®	tirita
Cardiac stimulant	medicamento para la circulación de la sangre
Chamomile, tincture of	tintura de manzanilla
Condom	preservativo, condón
Cotton	el algodón
Cough syrup	el jarabe contra la tos
Disinfectant	el desinfectante
Drops	las gotas
Ear drops	las gotas para los oídos
Elastic bandage	venda elástica
Eye droops	las gotas para los ojos
Gauze bandage	gasa
Insecticide	el insecticida
Insulin	insulina
Iodine, tincture of	tintura de yodo
Laxative	el laxante
Medicine, medication	medicina, medicamento
Non-aspirin painkiller	analgésico sin aspirina
Ointment	pomada
Ointment for burns	pomada para quemaduras
Painkillers	las pastillas contra el dolor

158

Powder	los polvos
Prescription	la receta
Remedy	remedio
Sedative	el tranquilizante
Sleeping pills	los somníferos
Sunburn	quemadura por el sol
Sunburn cream	crema para las quemaduras de sol
Suppositories	los supositorios
Tablet	pastilla, comprimido
Thermometer	termómetro
Throat lozenges	las pastillas para la garganta
Vitamin pills	pastillas de vitaminas

Product Enclosure

Instrucciones	**Directions**
indicaciones	Indications
contraindicaciones	Contraindications
efectos secundarios	Side effects
precaución de interacciones farmacológicas	Drug interation precautions
Dosis	**Dosage**
tomar una vez al día / varias veces al día...	Take . . . once/several times a day
un comprimido	1 tablet
veinte gotas	20 drops
un vaso graduado	1 dosage cup
antes de las comidas	before meals
después de las comidas	after meals
en ayunas	on an empty stomach
sin masticar y con líquidos	Take with water and swallow
disolver con un poco de agua	Dissolve in a little water
dejar deshacerse en la boca	Let dissolve in your mouth
aplicar una capa fina sobre la piel y friccionar	Apply sparingly to the skin and rub in
lactantes	Infants
niños menores de... años	Children under ... years
niños de 6 a 12 años	Children 6-12 years old
Niños mayores de 12 años a adultos	Children older than 12 years and adults
Mantenga fuera del alcance de los niños.	Keep out of reach of children

159

At the Doctor's Office

> also Traveling with Children

Can you recommend a(n) ....
¿Puede recomendarme un...

doctor?
médico?

optometrist?
oculista?

gynecologist?
ginecólogo?

ear, nose, and throat specialist?
otorrinolaringólogo?

dermatologist?
dermatólogo?

pediatrician
pediatra?

general practitioner?
médico (general)?

urologist?
urólogo?

dentist?
dentista?

Where is his/her practice?
¿Dónde está su consulta (*Am* el consultorio)?

Medical Complaints

What's the trouble?
¿Qué molestias siente?

I am running a temperature.
Tengo fiebre.

I don't feel well.
Me siento mal.

I often feel dizzy.
Me mareo con frecuencia.

I fainted.
Me he desmayado.

I have a very bad cold.
Estoy muy resfriado.

I have a headache/sore throat.
Tengo dolor de cabeza/dolor de garganta.

I have a cough.
Tengo tos.

160

I've been stung.
Tengo una picadura.

I've been bitten.
Tengo una mordedura.

I have an upset stomach.
Tengo una indigestión.

I have diarrhea.
Tengo colitis.

I am constipated.
Tengo estreñimiento.

The food doesn't agree with me. / I can't handle the heat.
La comida me hace mal. / El calor no me sienta bien.

I've hurt myself.
Me he hecho una herida.

I fell down.
Me he caído.

Could you give me/prescribe me something for …?
¿Podría usted darme/recetarme algo para…?

I usually take…
Normalmente tomo…

I have high/low blood pressure.
Tengo la presión sanguínea alta/baja.

I am a diabetic.
Soy diabético.

I am pregnant.
Estoy embarazada.

I had … recently.
Hace poco tuve…

Examination

What can I do for you?
¿Qué puedo hacer por usted?

Where does it hurt?
¿Dónde le duele?

It hurts here.
Me duele aquí.

Take off your clothes. / Roll up your sleeve, please.
Quítese la ropa. / Súbase la manga, por favor.

Take a deep breath. Hold your breath.
Respire profundamente. Contenga la respiración.

A blood/urine sample is necessary.
Es necesario un análisis de sangre/de orina.

You must rest in bed for a few days.
Debe quedarse en cama unos días.

It's nothing serious.
No es nada grave.

Do you have a vaccination card?
¿Tiene un certificado de vacunación?

I've been vaccinated against …
Estoy vacunado de/contra…

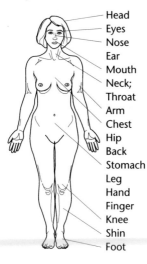

Head	cabeza
Eyes	los ojos
Nose	la nariz
Ear	oreja
Mouth	boca
Neck;	cuello;
Throat	garganta
Arm	brazo
Chest	pecho
Hip	cadera
Back	espalda
Stomach	el vientre
Leg	pierna
Hand	la mano
Finger	dedo
Knee	rodilla
Shin	espinilla
Foot	el pie

In the Hospital

How long will I have to stay here?
¿Cuánto tiempo tendré que quedarme aquí?

I cannot fall asleep.
No puedo dormirme.

Could you give me…
¿Podría darme…?

a glass of water.
un vaso de agua.

a pain killer.
un analgésico.

162

a sleeping pill.
un somnífero.

a hot-water bottle.
una bolsa de agua caliente.

When can I get up?
¿Cuándo podré levantarme?

Illnesses and Complaints

Abscess . . . . absceso
AIDS . . . . el sida
Alcoholism . . . . alcoholismo
Allergic to..., to be . . . . ser alérgico al...
Allergy . . . . alergia
Anorexia . . . . anorexia
Anxiety . . . . ansiedad
Appendicitis . . . . (la) apendicitis
Asthma . . . . el asma
Backaches . . . . (los) dolores de espalda
Blood poisoning . . . . la intoxicación de la sangre
Broken . . . . roto
Bronchitis . . . . la bronquitis
Bruise . . . . la contusión
Bulimia . . . . bulimia
Burn . . . . quemadura
Cancer . . . . el cáncer
Chest pain . . . . angina
Chills . . . . escalofríos
Cholera . . . . el cólera
Circulatory disorder . . . . (los) trastornos de la circulación
Cold . . . . resfriado (*Am* resfrío)
Colic . . . . cólico
Concussion . . . . la conmoción cerebral
Constipation . . . . estreñimiento
Contagious . . . . contagioso
Cramp . . . . el calambre, espasmo
Depression . . . . depresión
Diabetes . . . . la diabetes
Diarrhea . . . . diarrea
Difficulty breathing . . . . (las) dificultades de respiración
Diphtheria . . . . difteria
Dislocated . . . . dislocado
Dizziness . . . . mareo, vértigo
Fainting . . . . desmayo
Fever . . . . la fiebre
Flu . . . . la gripe
Food poisoning . . . . la intoxicación
Fracture . . . . fractura

Gas	flato, ventosidad
Hay fever	la fiebre del heno
Headache	dolor de cabeza
Heart attack	el ataque cardíaco; infarto cardíaco
Heart defect	defecto cardíaco
Heart trouble	(los) trastornos cardíacos
Heartburn	el ardor de estómago
Hemorrhage	hemorragia
Hemorrhoids	(las) hemorroides
Hernia	hernia
Herpes	el herpes
High blood pressure	hipertensión arterial
Hoarseness	ronquera
Hurt, to	herir
Illness	la enfermedad
Impaired balance	trastornos del equilibrio
Impaired vision	trastornos visuales
Indigestion	la indigestión
Infection	la infección
Inflammation	la inflamación
Injury	herida
Insomnia	insomnio
Jaundice	ictericia
Kidney stone	cálculo renal
Lumbago	lumbago
Malaria	malaria
Migraine	jaqueca
Miscarriage	aborto espontáneo
Nausea	(las) náuseas
Nephritis	la nefritis
Nosebleed	hemorragia nasal
Otitis	otitis
Pain	dolor
Pain on the side	dolor en el costado
Paralysis	la parálisis
Pneumonia	pulmonía
Poisoning	envenenamiento, la intoxicación
Polio	la polio(mielitis)
Pulled ligament	la distensión
Rash	la erupción cutánea
Rheumatism	el reumatismo
Rhinitis	rinitis, (*Am* resfrío)
Sciatica	ciática
Sinusitis	la sinusitis
Smallpox	viruela

Sore throat	el dolor de garganta
Stomachache	el dolor de estómago
Stroke	apoplejía, hemorragia cerebral
Sunburn	quemadura por el sol
Sunstroke	la insolación
Swelling	la hinchazón
Swollen	hinchado
Tachycardia	taquicardia
Tetanus	los tétanos
Tonsillitis	amigdalitis
Torn ligaments	rotura de ligamentos
Tumor	el tumor
Typhus	el tifus
Ulcer	úlcera
Venereal disease	la enfermedad venérea
Whooping cough	tosferina (*Am* la tos convulsa)
Wound	la herida, el corte
Yellow fever	la fiebre amarilla

Body—Doctor—Hospital

Abdomen	el abdomen
Anesthesia	anestesia
Ankle	tobillo
Appendix	el apéndice
Arm	brazo
Back	espalda
Bandages	(los) vendajes
Bladder	vejiga;
Bleed, to	sangrar
Blister	ampolla
Blood	la sangre
Blood group	grupo sanguíneo
Blood pressure	la presión de la sangre (alta/baja)
Bone	hueso
Bowel movement	la deposición
Brain	cerebro
Breathe	respirar
Bronchi	los bronquios
Bypass	la derivación
Cardiologist	cardiólogo
Certificate	certificado
Chest	pecho
Collarbone	clavícula
Consultation	consulta
Cough	la tos
Diagnosis	el diagnóstico

Diet	la dieta, el régimen
Digestion	la digestión
Disinfect, to	desinfectar
Dress, to	vendar
Ear	oído
Eardrum	tímpano
Esophagus	esófago
Examination	el examen
Eyes	los ojos
Face	cara, rostro
Finger	dedo
Foot	el pie
Gallbladder	la vesícula
Hand	la mano
Head	cabeza
Health insurance certificate .	el certificado del seguro de salud
Heart	el corazón
Hip	cadera
Hospital	el hospital, la clínica
Ill	enfermo
Infusion	la infusión
Injection	la inyección
Intestine	intestino
Joint	la articulación
Kidney	el riñón
Knee	rodilla
Leg	pierna
Lip	labio
Liver	hígado
Lung	el pulmón
Medical insurance	seguro de enfermedad
Menstruation	la menstruación, período
Mouth	boca
Muscle	músculo
Nail	uña
Neck	cuello
Nerve	nervio
Nervous	nervioso
Nose	la nariz
Nurse	enfermera
Operation	la operación
Pacemaker	el marcapasos
Pregnancy	embarazo
Prescribe, to	recetar, prescribir
Prosthesis	la prótesis
Pulse	pulso
Pus	el pus

Rib	costilla
Scar	la cicatriz
Sew, to	coser
Sexual organs	los órganos genitales
Shoulder	hombro
Skin	la piel
Specialist	el especialista
Spine	columna vertebral
Splint	tablilla, férula
Sting	picadura, pinchazo
Stomach	estómago; el vientre
Surgeon	cirujano/cirujana
Sweat, to	sudar
Throat	garganta
Tibia	tibia
Toe	el dedo del pie
Tomography	tomografía
Tongue	lengua
Tonsils	las amígdalas
Ultrasound scan	ecografía
Unconscious	desmayado, desvanecido
Urine	orina
Vaccination	vacuna
Vaccination card	el certificado de vacunación
Virus	el virus
Visiting hours	horario de visita
Vomit, to	vomitar, devolver
Waiting room	sala de espera
Ward	la sección
X-ray	radiografía
X-ray, to	hacer una radiografía

At the Dentist's

I have a toothache.
Tengo dolor de muelas.

This tooth (at the top/bottom/front/back) hurts.
Me duele esta muela (arriba/abajo/delante/atrás).

I have lost a filling.
He perdido un empaste (*Am* una tapadura).

I have broken a tooth.
Se me ha roto un diente.

It will only be a temporary job.
Se trata solamente de una cura provisional.

Give me an injection, please.
Póngame una inyección, por favor.

No injection, please.
No me ponga una inyección, por favor.

Bridge	puente
Cavity	agujero
Crown	corona
Filling	el empaste (*Am* la tapadura)
Gum	encía
Incisor	incisivo
Jaw	mandíbula
Molar	muela
Prosthesis	la prótesis
Take out, to	sacar
Tooth	el diente
Toothache	el dolor de muelas
Wisdom tooth	muela del juicio

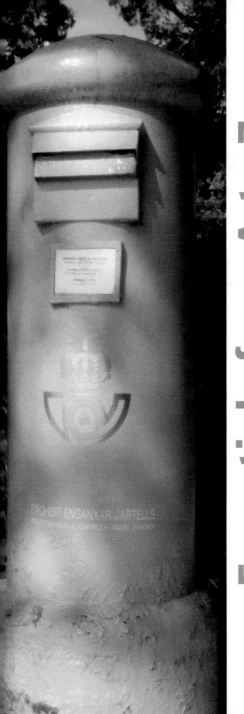

Essentials from A to Z

> **Your check card, please**
> You can pay without using cash almost everywhere nowadays.
> All common credit cards (MasterCard, Visa, American Express,
> etc.) are accepted everywhere.

Bank

Could you please tell me where the nearest bank is?
Por favor, ¿me podría decir dónde hay por aquí un banco?

I would like to exchange dollars into euros.
Quisiera cambiar dólares a euros.

Could you tell me what the exchange rate is today?
¿Podría decirme cómo está hoy el cambio?

I would like to cash...
Quisiera cobrar...

   this traveler's check.
   este cheque de viaje.

What is my credit card limit?
¿Cuál es el límite de mi tarjeta de crédito?

How many euros do I get for 100 dollars?
¿Cuántos euros recibiré por cien dólares?

May I see...
¿Puedo ver...

   your ID?
   su carnet de identidad?

   your passport?
   su pasaporte?

Sign here, please.
¿Quiere firmar aquí, por favor?

Amount	el importe, suma
ATM	cajero automático
Bank	banco
Bank account	cuenta bancaria
Bank charges	las comisiones
Bill	el billete (de banco)
Cable transfer	giro (postal)
Cash, in	al contado, en efectivo
Cent	cent
Change (small)	dinero suelto

170

Change, to	cambiar
Check	el cheque
make out a check	extender/librar un cheque
Checkbook	libro de cheques
Coin	moneda
Credit card	tarjeta de crédito
Currency	moneda
Euro	euro
Exchange	cambio
Exchange rate	tipo de cambio
Foreign currency	las divisas
Form	impreso, formulario
Money	dinero
Pay, to	pagar
Payment	pago
Pin number	número secreto, la clave
Receipt	recibo
Signature	firma
Swiss franc	franco suizo
Transfer	giro
wire transfer	giro telegráfico
Traveler's check	el cheque de viaje
Withdraw, to	retirar

Filming and Photographing

➤ also Photo Supplies

Would you mind taking a picture of us?
¿Sería tan amable de hacernos una fotografía?

That's very nice of you.
Es muy amable.

Just press this button.
Pulse este botón, por favor.

You set the distance/aperture like this.
La distancia/El diafragma se ajusta de esta forma.

May I take a picture of you?
¿Puedo fotografiarle/la?

This will be a nice reminder of our vacation.
Así tenemos un bonito recuerdo de nuestras vacaciones.

Camera	cámara fotográfica
Landscape format	formato apaisado
Photo	foto

Portrait format . . . . formato vertical
Snapshot . . . . una instantánea
Take photos, to . . . . fotografiar

Lost-and-Found Office

➢ also Police

Where is the lost and found office, please?
Por favor, ¿podría decirme dónde está la oficina de objetos perdidos?

I have lost…
He perdido…

I left my purse on the train.
He olvidado mi bolso en el tren.

Please let me know if it's handed in.
¿Sería tan amable de avisarme si lo encuentran?

Here's the address of my hotel/my home address.
Aquí tiene la dirección de mi hotel/de mi casa.

Police

Could you please tell me where the nearest police station is?
Por favor, ¿podría decirme dónde está la comisaría de policía más cercana?

I would like to report…
Quisiera denunciar…

a theft.
un robo.

a mugging.
un atraco.

They stole my…
Me han robado…

purse.
el bolso.

wallet.
billetera.

my camera.
mi cámara fotográfica.

my car/my bicycle.
mi coche / mi bicicleta.

172

My car was broken into.
Me han forzado la puerta del coche.

... was stolen from my car.
Me han robado... del coche.

I have lost...
He perdido...

My son/daughter is missing.
Ha desaparecido mi hijo / mi hija.

This man is harassing me.
Este hombre me está molestando.

Can you help me, please?
¿Puede usted ayudarme, por favor?

At exactly what time did this happen?
¿A qué hora exactamente ha sucedido?

Your name and address, please.
Por favor, su nombre y dirección.

Please get in touch with the American consulate.
Por favor, diríjase al consulado estadounidense.

Aggression	agresión
Arrest, to	arrestar
Beat up, to	golpear, pegar
Break into, to	forzar, violentar
Car radio	la radio del coche
Car registration	registro del vehículo
Check	el cheque
Coin purse	monedero
Confiscate, to	confiscar
Court	el tribunal
Credit card	tarjeta de crédito
Crime	el crimen
Documents	los documentos
Drug addiction	drogadicción
Drugs	las drogas
Fault	culpa
Harass, to	molestar, importunar
ID card	el carnet de identidad
Jail	la cárcel
Judge	el juez
Key	la llave
Lawyer	abogado
Lose, to	perder
Passport	el pasaporte

Pickpocket	ratero
Police	policía
Police car	el coche de policía
Police custody, to be in	estar bajo arresto
Police officer	el/la policía
Rape	la violación
Report, to	denunciar
Sexual harassment	acoso sexual
Smuggling	contrabando
Theft	robo
Thief	el ladrón

Post Office

Where is...
¿Dónde está...

the nearest post office?
la oficina de correos más cercana?

the nearest mailbox?
el buzón más cercano?

How much is a letter/postcard...
¿Cuánto cuesta una carta / una postal...

to the United States?
para Estados Unidos?

to the U.K.?
para el Reino Unido?

to Australia?
para Australia?

Three ...-euro stamps, please.
Tres sellos (*Am* estampillas) de... euros (pesos), por favor.

I would like to send this letter...
Quisiera enviar esta carta...

by airmail.
por correo aéreo.

by express mail.
por correo expreso.

How long does a letter to the U.S. take?
¿Cuánto tarda en llegar una carta a Estados Unidos?

Do you have collector's stamps?
¿Tiene sellos de coleccionista?

I would like to withdraw ... euros from my postal savings account.
Quisiera retirar... euros de mi cuenta de ahorro postal.

➢ also Bank

Address	la dirección
Addressee	destinatario
Airmail	por correo aéreo
Collection	recogida
Collector's stamp	sello de coleccionista
Customs declaration	la declaración de aduana
Declaration of value	la declaración de valor
Duty free	exento de impuestos
Envelope	el sobre
Express letter	carta expresa
Fax	el fax
Fill out, to	rellenar
Form	impreso, formulario
Forward, to	reexpedir, enviar
Letter	carta
Mailbox	el buzón
Mailing form	formulario de expedición
Main post office	Oficina Central de Correos
Money order	giro postal
Next day delivery	entrega al día siguiente
Package	el paquete
Post office	oficina de correos
Postage	franqueo
Postal savings account book	libreta de la caja (postal) de ahorros
Postcard	la postal
Poste restante	lista de correos (*Am* cartas detenidas)
Registered letter	carta certificada
Sender	el/la remitente
Small package	el paquete pequeño
Stamp	sello (*Am* estampilla)
Stamp, to affix a	franquear
Telegram	el telegrama
Telex	el télex
Weight	peso
Zip code	código postal

Telephoning

If you call Spain from the United States, you first need to dial 011-34, then the area code for the province (with the 9), and finally the number you want.
To place an international call from Spain, first dial 00, then the country code for the U.S. (1), then the appropriate area code, and the number you desire. The country code for England is 44, for Australia 61, and for New Zealand 64.

Could you tell me where the nearest phone booth is?
¿Podría decirme dónde está la cabina telefónica más cercana?

May I have a phone card, please?
Quisiera una tarjeta telefónica, por favor.

What is the area code for ...?
¿Cuál es el prefijo / el código territorial de..., por favor?

I would like to make a long-distance call to...
Una llamada a larga distancia con..., por favor.

I would like to make a collect call to...
Una llamada a cobro revertido, por favor.

Go to cabin number ..., please.
Pase a la cabina número...

A Telephone Conversation

A common way of addressing a caller is the Spanish equivalent of "Go ahead":
¿Diga?

Hello, who is speaking, please?
¿Con quién hablo, por favor?

Good morning, my name is...
Buenos días, me llamo...

May I speak to Mr./Mrs....?
¿Puedo hablar con el señor/la señora...?

I am sorry, he's not/she's not here/at home.
Lo siento, pero no está aquí/en casa.

Could he/she return my call?
Puede él/ella volver a llamar/llamar de vuelta?

Would you like to leave a message?
¿Desea usted dejar algún recado?

Please tell him/her that I called.
¿Podría decirle que he llamado?

The number you have reached is not in service.
El número de su llamada está equivocado.

Answer the phone, to	contestar el teléfono
Area code	prefijo
Busy	ocupado
Cell phone	teléfono móvil, celular
Charge	tarifa
Coin-operated phone	teléfono de monedas
Collect call	llamada a cobro revertido
Conference call	teleconferencia
Connection	conexión
Conversation	la conversación
Dial, to	marcar (el número)
Directory assistance	la información telefónica
International call	llamada internacional
Local call	llamada local
Long-distance call	llamada de larga distancia
Mobile phone	teléfono inalámbrico
Phone booth	cabina telefónica
Phone call	llamada telefónica
Phone card	tarjeta telefónica
Phone, to	llamar por teléfono, telefonear
Phone number	número de teléfono
Receiver	el receptor
Telephone	teléfono
Telephone answering machine	el contestador automático
Telephone directory	guía telefónica

Toilet and Bathroom

Where is the restroom, please?
¿Dónde está el baño, por favor?

May I use the restroom/bathroom, please?
¿Puedo usar el baño?

Could I have the key to the restroom, please?
¿Me da la llave del baño, por favor?

Clean	limpio
Dirty	sucio

Flush, to	largar el agua
Men (restroom)	Caballeros, Hombres
Restroom	baño, los servicios
Sanitary napkins	toallas higiénicas
Sink	lavabo
Soap	el jabón
Tampons	tampones
Toilet paper	el papel higiénico
Towel	toalla
Women (restroom)	Señoras

A Short Guide to Spanish Grammar

Definite and Indefinite Articles

		Definite article		Indefinite article	
Singular	masculine	**el** amigo	the friend	**un** amigo	a friend
	feminine	**la** rosa	the rose	**una** rosa	a rose
Plural	masculine	**los** amigos	the friends	**unos** amigos	friends
	feminine	**las** rosas	the roses	**unas** rosas	roses

An article is used with
● abstract nouns and nouns referring to tangible items when used in a general sense

¿Le gusta **el vino tinto**?	Do you like red wine?
Los perros son fieles.	Dogs are faithful.

● titles preceding last names (except when directly addressing the person)

el señor García	Mr. García

● certain names of cities ● sometimes with certain country names

La Habana, La Paz	**(el)** Uruguay, **(el)** Brasil, **(el)** Japón

No article is used with
● titles preceding first names ● terms of address

don José, **doña** Isabel	¿Qué tal, **señorita**?	How are you, Miss?

Singular and Plural Nouns

In Spanish, nouns are either masculine or feminine in gender:

● masculine nouns ending in –o, feminine ones in –a. Plural: + -s;
● masculine and feminine nouns ending in –e. Plural: + -s;
● plural of nouns ending in a *consonant* or in –í, ú: -es; (nouns ending in -ón, -l, -r are usually masculine) (nouns ending in –ión, -ad, -z are usually feminine):

Singular		Plural	
el libro	the book	los libros	the books
la mesa	the table	las mesas	the tables
el coche	the car	los coches	the cars
la lente	the lense	las lentes	the lenses
el árbol	the tree	los árboles	the trees
la nación	the nation	las naciones	the nations

Special features

● Some nouns can have a second meaning in the plural:
  el padre the father   los padres the parents

● Some nouns are used only in the plural:
  las gafas the (eye)glasses; los alrededores the environs

● Feminine nouns that begin with a stressed a use the article *el* in the singular, but *las* in the plural:
  el alma the soul, las almas; el águila the eagle, las águilas

Nominative – Accusative – Dative – Genitive

Nom. (Who? What?):	**El coche** corre.	The car is moving.
Acc. (Whom?):	Juan compra **el coche**.	Juan is buying the car.
Dative (To/for whom?) uses the preposition *a*:	Doy la mano **a mi amigo**.	I shake hands with my friend.
Genitive (Whose?) uses the preposition *de*:	El piso **de María** es caro.	Maria's apartment is expensive.

a + el = al	Voy **al** cine.	I'm going to the movies.
de + el = del	Viene **del** jardín.	He's coming from the garden

Preposition "de"

In Spanish, the preposition *de* is used

● to show the material of which a thing is made (where English uses adjectival nouns):
  mesa **de** mármol   marble table

● after nouns expressing quantity, size, or number:
  dos kilos **de** manzanas   two kilos of apples

● to denote origin, cause, or characteristics:
  Soy **de** Valencia.   I come from Valencia.
  María tiembla **de** miedo. Maria is trembling with fear.
  el mes **de** junio   the month of June

Diminutive Forms

- -ito, -cito, -ico, -illo:
  pajar**ito**, pajar**ico**, pajar**illo**   little bird
  un coche**cito**   a little car
- As an expression of endearment or to indicate liking:
  ¡Hola, Pedr**ito**!   Hi, Peter!

Adjectives

Singular and Plural

- Adjectives ending in –o form the feminine by adding –a:
  un jardín hermos**o**   a lovely garden
  una muchacha hermos**a**   a pretty girl

- Masculine adjectives ending in –or, án, ín, -ón form the feminine
  by adding an a:
  trabajad**or**, trabajad**ora**   industrious

- Adjectives of nationality: feminine form ends in –a
  (adjectives ending in –i, -e remain unchanged):
  español, español**a**   Spanish
  marroquí; árab**e**   Moroccan; Arabic

- Adjective plurals are formed in the same way as noun plurals:
  los chic**os** aleman**es**   the German boys

Agreement of Noun and Adjective

The adjective ending is always determined by the gender and
number of the noun it modifies:

el muchacho	**rubio**	the blond boy
la muchacha	**rubia**	the blond girl
los muchachos	**rubios**	the blond boys
las muchachas	**rubias**	the blond girls

Adverb

In addition to original adverbs: *pronto* (soon), *aquí* (here), there are
derived adverbs, which are formed by attaching –*mente* to the
feminine form or to an –*e* or final consonant of the adjective:

Lo he hecho **rápidamente**.   I did it quickly.
Leo **principalmente** novelas.   I read mainly novels.

Regular Comparison of Adjectives and Adverbs

caro	más caro	el más caro	carísimo
expensive	more expensive	most expensive	very expensive

Las rosas son **más caras** que los claveles.	Roses are more expensive than carnations.
Estas rosas son **carísimas / las más caras.**	These roses are very expensive/the most expensive.

Irregular Comparison

- Adjectives: *grande, mayor, más grande; pequeño, menor, más pequeño*
- Adverbs: *bien, mejor, muy bien; mal, peor, muy mal:*
  Me siento **mejor** / muy mal. I feel better/very bad.

Verb: Present Tense and Past Participle

a) ser – estar;   haber – tener

	ser	estar	to be	haber	tener	to have
yo	soy	estoy	I am	he	tengo	I have
tú	eres	estás	you are	has	tienes	you have
él			he is			he has
ella	es	está	she is	ha	tiene	she has
usted			you are			you have
nosotros, -as	somos	estamos	we are	hemos	tenemos	we have
vosotros, -as	sois	estáis	you are	habéis	tenéis	you have
ellos			they are			they have
ellas	son	están	they are	han	tienen	they have
ustedes			you are			you have
	sido	estado	been	(habido) tenido		had

- On the use of *ser* and *estar,* see page 188.
- *Haber* is used only for the compound tenses.
  Hemos comido bien. We have eaten well.
- The personal pronoun is used only if it is meant to be emphasized.
- As a polite form, use the 3rd person singular when speaking to one person, and the 3rd person plural when addressing more than one person:
  ¿Qué tal **está** usted, señor Pérez? How are you, Mister Pérez?
  ¿Qué tal **están** ustedes, señores? How are you, gentlemen?

b) Regular Verbs

There are three conjugations, or groups of verbs, in Spanish, based on the ending of the infinitive:

	-ar		-er	-ir
	hablar to speak		comprender to understand	recibir to receive
yo	hablo	I speak	comprendo	recibo
tú	hablas	you speak	comprendes	recibes
él ella usted	habla	he speaks she speaks you speak	comprende	recibe
nosostros, -as	hablamos	we speak	comprendemos	recibimos
vosotros, -as	habláis	you speak	comprendéis	recibís
ellos ellas ustedes	hablan	they speak they speak you speak	comprenden	reciben
	hablado	spoken	comprendido	recibido

Imperfect – Preterit – Present Perfect

	hablar	comprender	recibir
Imperfect	hablaba hablabas hablaba hablábamos hablabais hablaban	comprendía comprendías comprendía comprendíamos comprendíais comprendían	recibía recibías recibía recibíamos recibíais recibían

	hablar	comprender	recibir
Preterit	hablé hablaste habló hablamos hablasteis hablaron	comprendí comprendiste comprendió comprendimos comprendisteis comprendieron	recibí recibiste recibió recibimos recibisteis recibieron

Present perfect	he hablado	he comprendido	he recibido

- The imperfect is used primarily to describe a state, as well as for habitual or interrupted past actions.

- The preterit ("indefinido") is used to express completed past actions that occurred at a definite time or in a definite period of time.

Imperfect	Preterit
Cuando **iba** a dormirme, As I was starting to fall asleep,	**sonó** el teléfono. the telephone rang.
Quería ser médico He wanted to be a doctor,	pero no **terminó** la carrera. but he didn't finish his studies.

Present Perfect and Preterit

- The present perfect (always with the auxiliary *haber*) is used for completed past actions when they are connected **with the present**.

- The preterit ("indefinido"), in contrast, is used for actions that are connected **with the past**:

Present Perfect	Preterit
¿Ya **ha venido** Anita? Has Anita come yet?	Ayer **vi** a Juan en el concierto. Yesterday I saw Juan at the concert.

Future

hablar	leer	escribir
hablar**é**	leer**é**	escribir**é**
hablar**ás**	leer**ás**	escribir**ás**
hablar**á**	leer**á**	escribir**á**
hablar**emos**	leer**emos**	escribir**emos**
hablar**éis**	leer**éis**	escribir**éis**
hablar**án**	leer**án**	escribir**án**

Instead of the future forms, quite often the present tense of *ir* + a + infinitive is used to express the near future:

Voy a hablar con Pedro.   I'm going to talk to Pedro.

Conditional

hablaría	leería	escribiría
hablarías	leerías	escribirías
hablaría	leería	escribiría
hablaríamos	leeríamos	escribiríamos
hablaríais	leeríais	escribiríais
hablarían	leerían	escribirían

The conditional often is used in polite expressions:

¿**Podría** usted ayudarme?   Could you help me?

Imperative

a) Affirmative forms

	hablar		comer	escribir
you (fam. sing.)	habla	speak!	come	escribe
you (fam. pl.)	hablad	speak!	comed	escribid
you (pol. sing.)	hable	speak!	coma	escriba
you (pol. pl.)	hablen	speak!	coman	escriban

● In Latin America, "ustedes" is usually used instead of "vosotros."
Hablen más alto, niños.   Speak louder, children.

b) Negative forms

	hablar	comer	escribir
you (fam. sing.)	no hables	no comas	no escribas
you (fam. pl.)	no habléis	no comáis	no escribáis
you (pol. sing.)	no hable (usted)	no coma	no escriba
you (pol. pl.)	no hablen (ustedes)	no coman	no escriban

Important Irregular Verbs

conocer to know; to meet

Present:	conozco, conoces, conoce, conocemos, etc.

dar to give

Present:	doy, das, da, damos, dais, dan
Preterit:	di, diste, dio, dimos, disteis, dieron

decir to say   dicho said

Present:	digo, dices, dice, decimos, decís, dicen
Future:	diré, dirás, dirá, diremos, diréis, dirán
Preterit:	dije, dijiste, dijo, dijimos, dijisteis, dijeron
Conditional:	diría, dirías, diría, diríamos, diríais, dirían
Imperative:	di/no digas, decid/no digáis, (no) diga, (no) digan

estar to be

Present:	estoy, estás, está, estamos, estáis, están
Preterit:	estuve, estuviste, estuvo, estuvimos, etc.

haber to have (only as an auxiliary verb: *he* estado)

Present:	he, has, ha, hemos, habéis, han
Future:	habré, habrás, habrá, habremos, habréis, habrán
Preterit:	hube, hubiste, hubo, hubimos, hubisteis, hubieron
Conditional:	habría, habrías, habría, habríamos, etc.

hacer to make, to do   hecho made, done

Present:	hago, haces, hace, hacemos, hacéis, hacen
Future:	haré, harás, hará, haremos, haréis, harán
Preterit:	hice, hiciste, hizo, hicimos, hicisteis, hicieron
Conditional:	haría, harías, haría, haríamos, haríais, harían
Imperative:	haz/no hagas, haced/no hagáis, (no) haga, etc.

ir to go   ido gone

Present:	voy, vas, va, vamos, vais, van
Preterit:	fui, fuiste, fue, fuimos, fuisteis, fueron
Imperfect:	iba, ibas, iba, íbamos, ibais, iban
Imperative:	ve/no vayas, id/no vayáis, (no) vaya, (no) vayan

poder to be able; can; may

Present:	puedo, puedes, puede, podemos, podéis, pueden
Future:	podré, podrás, podrá, podremos, podréis, podrán
Preterit:	pude, pudiste, pudo, pudimos, etc.
Conditional:	podría, podrías, podría, podríamos, etc.

poner to put, place, lay   puesto put

Present:	pongo, pones, pone, ponemos, ponéis, ponen
Future:	pondré, pondrás, pondrá, pondremos, etc.
Preterit:	puse, pusiste, puso, pusimos, etc.
Conditional:	pondría, pondrías, pondría, pondríamos, etc.
Imperative:	pon/no pongas, poned/no pongáis, (no) ponga, (no) pongan

querer to want, desire; to like, love

Present:	quiero, quieres, quiere, queremos, queréis, quieren
Future:	querré, querrás, querrá, querremos, etc.
Preterit:	quise, quisiste, quiso, quisimos, etc.
Conditional:	querría, querrías, querría, querríamos, etc.

saber to know; to be able, know how to

Present:	sé, sabes, sabe, sabemos, sabéis, saben
Future:	sabré, sabrás, sabrá, sabremos, sabréis, sabrán
Preterit:	supe, supiste, supo, supimos, etc.
Conditional:	sabría, sabrías, sabría, sabríamos, etc.

ser to be   **sido** been

Present:	soy, eres, es, somos, sois, son
Preterit:	fui, fuiste, fue, fuimos, fuisteis, fueron
Imperfect:	era, eras, era, éramos, erais, eran
Imperative:	sé/no seas, sed/no seáis, (no) sea, (no) sean

tener to have, own; **tener que** to have to, must

Present:	tengo, tienes, tiene, tenemos, tenéis, tienen
Future:	tendré, tendrás, tendrá, tendremos, etc.
Preterit:	tuve, tuviste, tuvo, tuvimos, etc.
Conditional:	tendría, tendrías, tendría, tendríamos, etc.
Imperative:	ten/no tengas, tened/no tengáis, (no) tenga, etc.

venir to com

Present:	vengo, vienes, viene, venimos, venís, vienen
Future:	vendré, vendrás, vendrá, vendremos, etc.
Preterit:	vine, viniste, vino, vinimos, etc.
Conditional:	vendría, vendrías, vendría, vendríamos, etc.
Imperative:	ven/no vengas, venid/no vengáis, (no) venga, etc.

ver to see; **verse** to meet one another **visto** seen

Present:	veo, ves, ve, vemos, veis, ven
Imperfect:	veía, veías, veía, veíamos, veíais, veían

volver to return; to give back **vuelto** returned

Present:	vuelvo, vuelves, vuelve, volvemos, volvéis, vuelven
Imperative:	vuelve/no vuelvas, volved/no volváis, (no) vuelva, (no) vuelvan

Ser and Estar (to be)

(for conjugation, see pages 86, 97)

● *Ser* = natural or inherent and essentially lasting conditions
  Ser is used before predicate nouns
  Ser is used to show time of day, day of the week, occupation, relationship, nationality, religion:

Juan **es inteligente**.	Juan is intelligent.
Carmen **es médica**.	Carmen is a doctor.

● *Estar* = shows location or position (temporary or permanent)
  Estar = expresses a state or feeling
  Estar before an adjective or a participle, expresses an accidental or temporary condition or a resultant state:

Fernando **está en Berlín**.	Fernando is in Berlin.
La puerta **está abierta**.	The door is open.

Comparison of meanings of *ser* and *estar*

ser = essential characteristics	*estar* = condition
Luis **es un hombre enfermo**. Luis is a sick man.	María **está enferma**. María is ill.
Luis **es generoso**. Luis is generous.	María **está** muy **generosa**. María is (being) very generous (today).
Luis **es joven**. Luis is young.	María **está joven**. María looks young.

Personal Pronouns

Dative		Accusative		After a preposition	
me	me	**me**	me	sobre **mí**	about me
te	you	**te**	you	sobre **ti**	about you
	him	**le, lo**	him	sobre **él**	about him
le	her	**la**	her	sobre **ella**	about her
	you	**le, lo**	you	sobre **usted**	about you
nos	us	**nos**	us	sobre **nosotros**	about us
os	you	**os**	you	sobre **vosotros**	about you
	them	**les, los**	them	sobre **ellos**	about them
les	you	**las**	them	sobre **ellas**	about them
		les, los; las	you	sobre **ustedes**	about you

- The masculine accusative forms *le, les* are more common in Spain, while *lo, los* are used more in Latin America.

- Dative and accusative pronouns without a preposition always immediately precede the verb (dative always before accusative):
  ¿Quién **me** llama?   Who is calling me?
  Siempre **me lo** dice.   He always says it to me.

- After the preposition *con,* the 1st and 2nd person singular forms of the pronoun are *conmigo* and *contigo:*
  Ana viene hoy **conmigo**.   Ana is coming with me today.

- If a noun used as a direct or indirect object precedes the verb, the corresponding pronoun must be used as well:
  La maleta **la** lleva Pedro.   Pedro is carrying the suitcase.
  A Juan no **le** he dado dinero.   I haven't given any money to Juan.

Reflexive Pronouns and Reflexive Verbs

acostumbrarse   to get used to

yo	**me**	acostumbro	I get used to
tú	**te**	acostumbras	you get used to
él, ella usted	**se**	acostumbra	he, she gets used to you get used to
nosotros, -as	**nos**	acostumbramos	we get used to
vosotros, -as	**os**	acostumbráis	you get used to
ellos, ellas ustedes	**se**	acostumbran	they get used to you get used to

Possessive Pronouns

Unstressed form			Stressed form	
mi	trabajo	my work	**mío, mía, míos, mías**	mine
tu	amigo	your friend	**tuyo, tuya, -os, -as**	{ yours his
su	jardín	{ his garden her garden your garden	**suyo, suyas, -os, -as**	{ hers yours
nuestro	padre	our father	**nuestro, nuestra, -os, -as**	ours
vuestro	tren	your train	**vuestro, vuestra, -os, -as**	yours
su	coche	{ their car your car	**suyo, suya, -os, -as**	{ their yours

Relative Pronouns

- *Que,* the most common relative pronoun, does not change.
- The definite article often precedes *que* after a preposition:
  Tengo el libro **que** buscas.   I have the book that you're looking for.
  El diccionario **con el que** traduzco. The dictionary with which I translate.
- *Quien, quienes* (for persons): almost exclusively after prepositions.
- *Lo que* = that which, what, which:
  El amigo **con quien** viajo.   The friend with whom I'm traveling.
  Dice siempre **lo que** piensa.   He always says what he thinks.

Demonstrative Pronouns

este / ese / aquel	libro	this book, that one, that one over there
esta / esa / aquella	flor	this flower, that one, that one over there
estos / esos / aquellos	vasos	these glasses, those, those over there
estas / esas / aquellas	blusas	these blouses, those, those over there
esto / eso / aquello		this, that, that (farther away)

Negation

- *No* (no, not) always precedes the verb.
- *Nada* (nothing) usually follows the verb. *Nadie, ninguno, nunca* (nobody, no one, never) follow or precede the verb.
- If *nada, nadie, ninguno, nunca* follow the verb, *no* must precede the verb.
  Este chico **no** aprende **nada**.   This boy isn't learning anything.
  ¿**No** tienes **ninguna** foto de él?   Don't you have any photo of him?

Spanish – English Glossary

A

a to
a causa de because of
a corto plazo on short notice
a diario every day
a esta hora about this time
a la derecha to the right
a la izquierda to the left
a menudo often
a nosotros to us
a partir de since
a tiempo on time
a través de through
a veces sometimes
abadía abbey
abandonar abandon, to
abdomen abdomen
abeja bee
abierto open
abogado lawyer
aborto involuntario
  miscarriage
abrelatas (el) can opener
abreviatura abbreviation
abridor (el) opener
abrigo coat
abril April
abrir open, to
absceso abscess
abuela grandmother
abuelo grandfather
aburrido bored
acá here
acampar camp, to
accesibilidad accessibility
accesible para sillas de
  ruedas wheelchair accessible
accidente accident

aceite oil
aceite de oliva olive oil
aceite solar suntan oil
aceituna olive
aceptar accept, to
acidez estomacal heartburn
aclimatarse acclimated, to get
acompañante (el/la)
  companion
acompañar accompany, to
acondicionador de aire (el)
  air conditioner
acoplado trailer
acoso sexual sexual harassment
acostarse go to bed, to; lie
  down, to
acto act
actor/actriz actor/actress
acuarela watercolor
acumulador battery (car)
adaptador (el) adapter
adecuado adequate
¡Adelante! Come in!
adelante forward
además besides
adentro inside
adicional additional
administración (la)
  administration
administración (la)
  management
aduana customs
adulto adult
advertir notice, to
aerobic (el) aerobics
aerodeslizador hovercraft
aeropuerto airport
afirmar maintain, to
afuera outside

agencia agency
agencia de viajes travel agency
agosto August
agotado exhausted
agradable pleasant
agradar please, to
agradecer thank, to
agresión aggression
agrio sour
agua caliente hot water
agua (el) water
agua fría cold water
agua mineral mineral water
agua potable drinking water
aguacate (el) avocado
aguafuerte (el) etching
aguja needle
agujero hole
ahora now
ahumado smoked
aire air
ajo garlic
al contrario on the contrary
al cuadrado squared
al este de east of
al frente de in front of
al máximo at most
al norte de north of
al oeste de to the west of
al sur de south of
al vapor steamed
ala wing
alambre (el) wire
alargar extend, to
alarma de incendio fire alarm
albahaca basil
albaricoque (el) apricot
albornoz (el) bathrobe
alcachofa artichoke
alcohol (el) alcohol
alegre cheerful
alergia allergy
aletas de natación swim fins

algo something; some
algodón (el) cotton
alguien somebody
alguna(s); alguno(s) some
alimento food
aliño dressing (food)
allá over there
allí there
almacén de vinos liquor store
almacén (el) grocery store
almeja clam
almendras almonds
almohada pillow
alojamiento lodging
alquilar rent, to
alquiler rent
alrededor de about
alrededores surroundings
alta tensión high voltage
altar (el) altar
altavoz speaker
¡Alto! Stop!
alto high; tall
altura height
amable nice
amar love, to
amargo bitter
amarillo yellow
ambos both
ambulancia ambulance
America America
americano American
amigdalitis (la) tonsilitis
amigo friend
amigo de juego playmate
amistoso friendly
amor love
ampolla blister
añadir add
analgésico analgesic; painkiller
ananás *(Am.)* pineapple
ancho broad, wide
Andalucía Andalusia

andaluz Andalusian
andén (el) train platform
anestesia anesthesia
anfiteatro amphitheater
anfitrión/anfitriona
  host/hostess
angina angina
angosto narrow
anguila eel
anillo ring
animal animal
animales domésticos
  domestic animals
año year
Año Nuevo New Year
año próximo, el next year
anotar write down, to
anteayer day before yesterday
antes before
antibiótico antibiotic
anticonceptivo contraceptive
anticongelante (el) antifreeze
antiguo ancient
anual annual
anular annul, to
anunciar announce, to
apartamento *(Am.)* apartment
apellido surname
apenas barely
apendicitis appendicitis
apetito appetite
apio celery
aplauso applause
apoplejía stroke
aprender learn, to
aprender un idioma learn a
  language, to
aproximadamente
  approximately
aquel, aquella that, that one
aquellos, aquellas those, those
  ones
aquí here

árbol (el) tree
arco arch
área de reposo rest area
área de servicios service area
área para asolearse (el)
  sunbathing area
arenque herring
aretes earrings
Argentina Argentine
argentino Argentinean
armario closet
aro de natación swimming ring
arqueología archeology
arquitecto (el/la) architect
arquitectura architecture
arreglar fix, to
arrendar rent, to
arresto arrest
arriba up
arroz rice
arte (el) art
artes gráficas graphic art
artes industriales (las)
  industrial arts
articulación (la) joint
artículos de cuero leather
  goods
artículos de papelería
  stationery
arveja pea
asado roasted
ascensor (el) elevator
asidero grip
asiento seat
asiento junto a la ventanilla
  window seat
asistencia de emergencia en
  carretera emergency road
  service
asma asthma
asociación (la) association
aspirina aspirin
asustar scare, to

ataque attack
ataque cardíaco (el) heart attack
atención attention
aterrizaje landing
atestado crowded
Atlántico Atlantic
atleta (el/la) athlete
atletismo track and field
atracar en land at, to
atrás back
atún tuna
aunque although
auriculares (los) headphones
ausente absent
auténtico authentic
auto- self-
autobús bus
autobús de aeropuerto shuttle bus
autobús urbano city bus
autodisparador self-timer
automático automatic
automóvil (el) car
autopista highway
autoridad (la) authority
autoservicio self-service
autotrén (el) car train
auxiliar de vuelo flight attendant
avería breakdown
aviso announcement
avispa wasp
ayer yesterday
ayuda help
ayuda de carretera highway help
ayuda para subir boarding assistance
ayudar help, to
ayuno fasting
ayuntamiento city hall
azafrán saffron

azúcar sugar
azul blue
azul claro (el) light blue
azul oscuro dark blue

B

badminton (el) badminton
bahía bay
bailar dance, to
bailarín/bailarina dancer
baile (el) ball (dance)
bajar go down, to
bajo below; low; small (height)
balcón (el) balcony
balet (el) ballet
balneario beach resort
baloncesto basketball
balonmano (el) handball
banco bank
banda band
bañera bathtub
banquetes a domicilio catering
bar (el) bar
barandilla handrail
barato cheap
barba beard
barra de chocolate chocolate bar
barrera barrier
barrio district
barroco Baroque
bastante enough
bastón cane
bastoncito de algodón cotton swab
bastones de esquí ski poles
basura garbage
baúl (el) trunk
bebé (el/la) baby
beber drink, to

bebida drink

beige beige

berenjena eggplant

besar kiss, to

beso kiss

betún (el) shoe polish

biberón feeding bottle

bicicleta bicycle

bicicleta de carrera racing bike

bicicleta de montaña mountain bike

bicicleta manual hand-operated bike

bidón water canister

bien good

bien asado well done

bien cocido/asado done

Bienvenido. Welcome.

bigote mustache

bikini (el) bikini

billete/abono semanal weekly ticket

billete de ida y vuelta (el) round-trip ticket

billete (el) ticket; bill

billetera wallet

bisutería fashion jewelry

bizantino Byzantine

blanco white

blando soft

blazer (el) blazer

blues (el) blues

blusa blouse

boca mouth

bocadillo sandwich

bocado snack

bocina horn (car)

boda wedding

bolear bowl, to

boletería ticket counter

boletín meteorológico weather report

boleto ticket

boleto multiviaje multitrip ticket

boleto por medio precio half-price ticket

bolígrafo ballpoint pen

boliviano Bolivian

bolsa bag

bolsa de basura garbage bag

bolsa de plástico plastic bag

bolsillo pocket

bolsita congelable freezer pack

bolsita de té tea bag

bolso purse

bomba de aire air pump

bomba de gasolina gas pump

bombero firefighter

bombilla eléctrica lightbulb

bombona de gas gas canister

bordado embroidery

borracho drunk

bosque forest

botas boots

botas de goma rubber boots

botas para esquiar ski boots

bote de paletas paddleboat

bote de remos rowboat

bote inflable rubber boat

bote salvavidas lifeboat

botella bottle

botella de oxígeno oxygen bottle

botillería liquor store

boutique (la) boutique

bóveda vault

braga panty

braille (el) braille

brasileño Brazilian

brazalete (el) bracelet

brocha de afeitar shaving brush

broche (el) pin

195

bronce (el) bronze
bronquios bronchial tubes
bronquitis (la) bronchitis
brújula compass
bucear dive, to
buen estado físico fit
bueno good
bufanda scarf
bufete de ensaladas diversas (el) salad bar
bufete libre para desayunar (el) breakfast buffet
bujía spark plug
bungalow (el) bungalow
burro donkey
buscar search, to
buzón (el) mailbox

C

caballa mackerel
Caballeros (sign) Men (sign)
caballo horse
cabaña hut
cabaré (el) cabaret, nightclub
cabeza head
cabina cabin
cabina para personas en silla de ruedas cabin for wheelchair users
cabina telefónica phone booth
cable de remolque (el) tow rope
cables para encendido jumper cables
cada every; each
cada hora every hour
cadera hip
caer fall, to
café (el) coffee
cafetera coffeemaker
caja box

caja de cambios gearbox
caja de caudales safe (box)
caja de enchufe outlet
cajero automático ATM
cajón box
cajón de arena sandbox
calabaza pumpkin
calamar squid
calambre cramp
calcetín sock
calculadora de bolsillo pocket calculator
calcular calculate, to
cálculo renal kidney stone
calefacción central (la) central heating
calidad quality
cálido warm
calienta-biberones (el) bottle warmer
caliente hot
calle (la) street
calle lateral sidestreet
calle principal main street
calma calm
calmante (el) sedative
calmarse calm down, to
calor heat
calzoncillos briefs
cama bed
cámara camera
cámara digital digital camera
cámara fotográfica camera
cámara submarina underwater camera
camarera waitress
camarero waiter
camarón shrimp
cambiar change, to
cambiar un vuelo change a flight, to
cambio change; exchange
cambio de aceite oil change

camcórder (la) camcorder
caminar walk, to
camino road
camión truck
camisa shirt
camiseta undershirt
campanario bell tower
camping (el) camping
campo field
campo de deportes athletic field
caña de pescar fishing rod
canadiense Canadian
canal (el) canal
cancelar cancel, to
cáncer (el) cancer
cancha de fútbol soccer field
canción (la) song
canguro (el/la) babysitter
canoa canoe
cansado tired
cantante (el/la) singer
cantar sing, to
cantidad amount
capilla chapel
capital (la) capital
capitán captain
capó hood
cápsula capsule
cara face
caramelos bonbons
caravana trailer home
carbón de parrilla charcoal
cárcel (la) jail
cargador porter
cargador de pilas battery charger
cariñoso gentle
carnaval carnival
carne meat
carne de cerdo pork
carne de cordero mutton
carne de res beef

carne de ternera veal
carne picada ground meat
carnet de conducir driver's license
carnet de identidad ID
carnet de vacuna (el) vaccination card
carnet náutico (el) boating license
carnicería butcher shop
caro expensive
carpa tent
carretera highway
carro portaequipajes baggage cart
carta letter
carta certificada registered letter
carta urgente special delivery letter
cartel poster
cartera billfold; purse
cartucho de gas gas cartridge
casa house
casa de vacaciones vacation home
casa flotante houseboat
casa rodante trailer home
casado married
casarse get married, to
casco helmet
casco de bicicleta bike helmet
casero homemade
casete (el) cassette
casi almost
casino casino
caspa dandruff
castellano Castilian
castigo punishment
Castilla Castile
castillo castle
castillo de arena sand castle
casualidad coincidence

catalán Catalonian
Cataluña Catalonia
catarata waterfall
catedral (la) cathedral
causa cause
causar cause, to
cebolla onion
cementerio cemetery
cena dinner
cenicero ashtray
centímetro centimeter
central central
centro center; downtown
centro de gimnasia fitness
  center
cepillo brush
cepillo de dientes toothbrush
cepillo para calzado shoe
  brush
cepillo para fregar washing-up
  brush
cerámica pottery
cerca (de) near; close to
cercano close by
cereal cereal
cerebro brain
cereza cherry
cerrado closed
cerrar con llave lock, to
certificado certificate
certificar certify, to
cerveza beer
cerveza sin alcohol
  nonalcoholic beer
césped (el) lawn
cesto basket
chaleco vest
chaleco salvavidas life jacket
champán (el) champagne
champú (el) shampoo
chaqueta jacket
chaqueta de cuero leather
  jacket

cheque de viaje traveler's
  check
chicle chewing gum
chico little
chileno Chilean
chiste joke
chocolate chocolate
choque crash
chubasco rain shower
chupete nipple; pacifier
cicatriz scar
ciclismo cycling
ciego blind
cielo sky
cielo raso ceiling
ciertamente surely
cierto certain (true); sure
cigarrería tobacco store
cigarrillo cigarette
cigarro cigar
cine (el) movie theater
cinturón belt
cinturón de seguridad safety
  belt
circo circus
ciruela plum
cirujano surgeon
cisterna cistern
cita appointment
ciudad (la) city
ciudad vieja (la) historical
  district
claro clear
clase (la) class; sort
clásico classic
clásico del cine movie classic
clavícula collarbone
clavija de enchufe plug
clavo nail
cliente customer
clima (el) climate
club nocturno nightclub
coche-cama sleeper car

coche (el) car
coche policial police car
coche restaurante dining car
coche todo terreno SUV
cocina kitchen
cocina de gas gas stove
cocinar cook, to
cocinero cook
coco coconut
código de puerta door code
código postal zip code
coger grab, to
colchón mattress
colchón de aire air mattress
coleccionar collect, to
colega (el/la) colleague
cólera (el) cholera
cólico colic
coliflor (la) cauliflower
colina hill
collar necklace
colombiano Colombian
colores, de colored
columna column
columna vertebral spine
comedia comedy
comedia musical musical comedy
comedor dining room
comenzar begin, to
comer eat, to
comerciante de objetos de arte art dealer
comestible edible
cómico comedian
comida food; meal
comida de bebé baby food
comida frita fried food
comida principal entree
comino cumin
comisión bancaria (la) bank charge
como as; like

cómo how
cómodo comfortable
compañero fellow
compañía aérea airline
compartimiento compartment
compartimiento de no fumadores (el) non-smoking compartment
competencia contest
compositor composer
comprar buy, to
comprender understand, to
computadora portátil laptop
común common
con with
con gusto gladly
concierto concert
concierto sinfónico symphonic concert
condimento seasoning
condón condom
conducir drive, to
conductor (el) conductor
conejo rabbit
conexión (la) connection
confianza confidence
confirmar confirm, to
confiscar confiscate, to
confitería candy store
confundir con mistake for, to
conmoción cerebral (la) concussion
conocer know, to
conocer a alguien know somebody, to
conocido well-known
conocido(a) acquaintance
conservar keep, to; conserve, to
conservas canned goods
consigna de equipaje baggage deposit
consistir en consist of, to
consulado consulate

consulta consultation

consumo de agua water consumption

contacto contact

contagioso contagious

contar tell, to; count, to

contenido content

contento happy; pleased; glad

contestador telefónico, el answering machine

contestar answer, to

contra against

contrabando smuggling

contrato contract

control de pasaporte passport control

control de seguridad security check

control por radar radar control

controlar control, to

contusión bruise

convenir agree, to

convento convent

conversación (la) conversation

conversar converse, to

copa para vino wine glass

copia copy

copos de avena rolled oats

corazón heart

corbata necktie

cordero lamb

cordial cordial

cordón cord

cordón de empalme extension cord

cordones shoelaces

coro choir

corona crown

correcto correct; right

correo aéreo airmail

correr run, to

corriente current

cortadura cut

corte escalado layered cut

cortés polite

corto short

cortocircuito short circuit

cortometraje (el) short film

cosa thing

coser sew, to

costa coast; shore

costar cost, to

costarricense Costa Rican

costilla chop

costo por kilómetro cost per kilometer

creativo creative

creer believe, to

crema cream

crema para las manos hand cream

crema solar sun cream

crimen crime

cristal (el) crystal

cristianismo Christianity

cristiano Christian

cruce (el) crossing

crucero cruise

crudo raw

cruz (la) cross

cuaderno notebook

cuaderno para colorear coloring book

cuadrado square

cuadro painting

cuando when

cuartel de bomberos fire department

cuarto room

cuarto de baño bathroom

cubierta deck

cubiertos (los) silverware

cubo de la basura garbage can

cuchara spoon

cucharita teaspoon

cuchillo knife

cuello neck
cuenta bill
cuenta bancaria bank account
cuerda rope
cuerda de carpa tent rope
cuerda de la ropa clothesline
cuerpo body
cueva cave
¡Cuidado! Caution!
cuidado care
cuidadosamente carefully
cuidar look after, to
cuidar a take care of, to
culebra snake
culpa guilt
cultura culture
cumbre (la) summit
cumpleaños (el) birthday
cumplir con fulfill, to
cuna crib
cuñada sister-in-law
cuñado brother-in-law
cúpula dome
curioso curious
curso course
cursos de esquí skiing lessons
cursos de natación swimming
  lessons
curva curve

D

Damas Women (sign)
dañar damage, to
daño damage
dar give, to
dar la vuelta turn back, to
darse cuenta become aware, to
darse prisa, apurarse hurry,
  to
dátil date (fruit)
datos personales personal data

de from; of
de colores colored
de mala gana reluctantly
de paso passing through
de repente suddenly
¿De veras? Really?
de vez en cuando from time to
  time
debajo under
deber have to, to
débil weak
decidir decide, to
decir say, to
declaración de aduana
  customs declaration
declaración de valor
  declaration of value
declaración (la) statement
dedo finger
dedo del pie toe
defecto defect
definitivamente definitively
definitivo definitive; final
dejar leave, to
delante in front
delante de in front of
deletrear spell, to
delgado thin
delicioso delicious
dentro inside
denunciar denounce, to
departamento de
  fumadores smoking
  compartment
deporte sport
deposición bowel movement
depositar deposit, to
depósito deposit
derecho fee; right; straight
derecho de aduana duty
  (customs)
derechos de aeropuerto
  airport tax

desagradable unpleasant
desarrollar develop, to
desayunar breakfast, to
desayuno breakfast
descansar rest, to
descanso rest
desconocido unknown
describir describe, to
descubrir discover, to
descuento para niños children discount
desde from; of; since
desde hace since
desear want, to; wish, to
desembocar lead into, to
desempleado unemployed
desfiladero gorge
desfile parade
desgracia misfortune
desgraciadamente unfortunately
desilusionado disappointed
desinfectante (el) disinfectant
desinfectar disinfect, to
desmayo faint
desnudo naked; nude
desodorante (el) deodorant
despedirse say good-bye, to
despegue (el) takeoff
despertador alarm clock
despertar wake up, to (s.o.)
despertarse wake up, to (oneself)
despierto awake
después afterwards
destelladores de emergencia emergency blinkers
destinatario addressee
desvío detour
detenerse stop, to
detergente (el) detergent
detrás behind
deuda debt

devolver bring back, to
día de llegada day of arrival
día (el) day
día laborable workday
diabetes (la) diabetes
diagnosis diagnóstico
diario daily
diarrea diarrhea
dibujar draw, to
dibujo drawing
diciembre December
diente tooth (front)
dieta diet
diferente different
difícil difficult
dificultad de respirar (la) difficulty breathing
difteria diphtheria
digestión digestion
dínamo dynamo
dinastía dynasty
dinero money
dinero suelto change (money)
Dios God
dique (el) dam
dirección direction; address; management
dirección del viento wind direction
directamente directly
directo direct
director director
director de orquesta orchestra conductor
dirigido por directed by
disco compacto compact disc
discoteca discotheque
disculparse excuse oneself, to
dislocado dislocated
disparador shutter
distancia distance
distensión muscular pulled muscle

distinguido distinguished
distribuidora automática vending machine
diversión fun
divertirse fun, to have
divisas foreign currency
doble double
doble (el) doubles
documental (el) documentary
documentos documents
documentos del vehículo vehicle documentation
doler hurt, to
dolor de cabeza headache
dolor de espalda backache
dolor de garganta (el) sore throat
dolor de muelas toothache
domicilio place of residence
domingo Sunday
dorado golden
dormir sleep, to
dormitorio bedroom
drama (el) drama
ducha shower
ducha con asiento shower seat
dueño owner
dueño de casa man of the house
dulce sweet
dulces candy
duradero durable
durante during
durante el día during the day
durar last, to
duro hard

E

echar de menos miss, to
edad (la) age
Edad Media Middle Ages

edificio building
efectivo cash
efectivo, en in cash
ejemplo example
ejemplo, por example, for
ejercicios de desarrollo muscular bodybuilding
él he
el (or la or lo) mejor best
elástico para el pelo hair band
eléctrico electric(al)
elegir choose, to
ella she
ellos; ellas they
embajada embassy
embalaje packing
embarazo pregnancy
embotellamiento traffic jam
embrague clutch
embutido sausage meat
emergencia emergency
empapado soaked
empaquetar pack, to
emparentado related (by blood)
empaste filling (tooth)
empatar tie, to (sports)
empate (el) tie (sports)
emperador/emperatriz emperor/empress
empezar begin, to
emplear hire, to
empleo job
empresa business
en on, in, at
en camino on the way
en casa at home
en caso de que in case that
en ninguna parte nowhere
en otra parte elsewhere
en realidad actually
en todas partes everywhere
en una semana in a week
en vez de instead of

encantador charming
encendedor (el) lighter
encender light, to
encendido ignition
encía gum
encontrar find, to
encontrarse meet, to
endulzador sweetener
enero January
enfadarse angry, to get
enfermedad infantil childhood disease
enfermedad (la) illness
enfermera nurse
enfermo sick
engaño swindle
enojado angry
enseñar teach, to
entonces also; then
entorno environment
entrada entrance
entrar come in, to
entre among; between
entrega de equipaje baggage claim
entrega de llaves return of the keys
entregar leave, to; hand in, to
entremeses hors d'oeuvre
entrenamiento training
entretenimiento entertainment
entusiasmado (con) enthusiastic (about)
envenenamiento poisoning
envenenamiento de la sangre blood poisoning
enviar send, to
epilepsia epilepsy
época period
equipaje (el) luggage
equipo team
equipo de buceo diving equipment

equipo para reparar neumáticos tire repair kit
equivocación mistake
equivocarse miscalculate, to; make a mistake, to
errar miss, to
error (el) mistake
erupción cutánea (la) skin rash
erupción (la) rash
escala stopover
escalar rock climbing
escalera ladder
escalinata stairs
escalofrío shiver
escaparate (el) store window
escarola endive
escarpado steep
escoger choose, to
escolares schoolchildren
escribir write, to
escritura writing
escritura a mano handwriting
escuchar listen, to
escuchar música listen to music, to
escuela school
escuela de equitación riding school
escultor sculptor
escultura sculpture
ese, esa that, that one
esófago esophagus
esos, esas those, those ones
espacio space
espalda back
España Spain
español Spaniard
español Spanish
espárrago asparagus
especia spice
especial special
especialidad specialty

especialmente especially

espectáculo performance; show

espectáculo folclórico folk concert

espectador spectator

espejo mirror

espejo retrovisor rearview mirror

esperar wait, to

espinaca spinach

esposa wife

espuma de afeitar shaving cream

esquí a campo traviesa cross-country skiing

esquí acuático waterski

esquí (el) ski

esquiar ski, to

esquina corner

esta mañana this morning

esta tarde this evening

estable stable

estaca de carpa tent peg

estación season

estación central (la) main train station

estación de autobuses bus station

estación de esquí (la) ski station

estación de trenes (la) train station

estación final (la) end of the line

estacionamiento parking

estacionar park, to

estadía, estancia stay

estadio stadium

estado state

Estados Unidos United States

estadounidense U.S. national

estampilla *(Am.)* stamp

estampilla (la) postage stamp

estar be, to

estar a favor de be in favor of, to

estar acostumbrado be used to, to

estar apurado be in a hurry, to

estar complacido be pleased, to

estar de pie stand, to

estar en contra de be against, to

estar hambriento be hungry, to

estar interesado en be interested in, to

estar mareado be seasick, to

estar sorprendido de be surprised at, to

estatua statue

este east

estilo style

estimulante cardíaco cardiac stimulant

estómago stomach

estornudar sneeze, to

estrecho narrow

estrella star

estreñimiento constipation

estreno premiere

estropeado spoiled

estudiar study, to

estufa eléctrica electric stove

euro euro

Europa Europe

europeo European

exactamente exactly

examen (el) examination

excavación (la) excavation

excelente excellent

excepto except

excursión tour

excursión de un día (la) day trip

excursión en bicicleta cycling tour

excursión en velero sailing trip
excursión (la) excursion
excursión por la ciudad city sightseeing
excusa excuse
exento de derechos de aduana duty-free
expedir forward, to
expendedor de sellos stamp machine
exposición (la) exhibition
expresión (la) expression
expresionismo expressionism
expreso express
exterior exterior
extintor (el) fire extinguisher
extra extra
extranjero foreigner
extraordinario extraordinary
extraviarse get lost, to

F

fábrica factory
fácil easy
factor de protección solar sun protection factor (SPF)
factura invoice
falda skirt
falso false
falta mistake
faltar miss, to
familia family
famoso famous
farmacia pharmacy
faro lighthouse
faros headlights
fatigoso strenuous
fax (el) fax
faxear fax, to
febrero February
fecha date

fecha de nacimiento birthdate
felicidad (la) happiness
felicitación (la) congratulation
feliz happy
feo ugly
feria fair
ferretería hardware store
ferrocarril de cremallera cog railroad
festival (el) festival
fiambre (el) cold cut
fiambrería delicatessen
fiebre del heno (la) hay fever
fiebre (la) fever
fiesta party
fijación de los esquís ski binding
fijador para el pelo (el) setting lotion
filmadora video camera
fin de semana (el) weekend
fin (el) end
finalmente finally
finca farm
fino thin
firma signature
firmar sign, to
firme firm; tough
flaco skinny
flequillo bang
flor (la) flower
florero vase
floristería flower shop
flotadores de brazos water wings
folclore (el) folklore
folleto brochure
forma form (shape)
formato apaisado landscape format
formato vertical portrait format
formulario form (document)
fortaleza fortress

fósforo match
foto photo
fotografía photograph
fotografiar take pictures, to
fotómetro (el) light meter
fotosensibilidad (la) film speed
fractura fracture
franquear stamp, to
franqueo postage
frase sentence
fraude (el) fraud
frazada blanket
frecuentemente frequently
fregadero sink (kitchen)
freno brake
freno de emergencia emergency brake
freno manual handbrake
frente front
fresa strawberry
fresco fresh
frío cold
frontera border
fruta fruit
fuego fire
fuegos artificiales fireworks
fuente (la) fountain; spring
fuera de outside; away
fuera de estación off-season
fuera de juego offside
fuerte strong
fumador smoker
fumar smoke, to
función performance
funcionar function, to
funicular cable railway
furgón van
furioso furious
fusible (el) fuse
fútbol americano football
fútbol (el) soccer
futuro future

G

gafas de esquí ski goggles
galería gallery
Galicia Galicia
gallego Galician
galletas cookies; crackers
gambas shrimp
ganancia profit
ganar win, to
gancho hook
garaje (el) garage
garantía guarantee
garbanzos chickpeas
garganta throat
garrafa carafe
gas (el) gas
gasa gauze
gastar spend, to
gastos expenses
gastos adicionales additional expenses
gato cat; jack
gaviota seagull
gel de ducha shower gel
gel para el pelo (el) hair gel
general general
género material (fabric)
gente (la) people
genuino genuine
gerente manager
gimnasia gymnastics
giro bancario bank draft
giro postal cable transfer; money order
giro telegráfico wire transfer
glucosa glucose
gobierno government
golf (el) golf
golpear beat up, to
gordo fat
gorra cap
gorro de baño bathing cap

gota drop
gotas para los oídos eardrops
gotas para los ojos (las) eyedrops
gótico Gothic
gozar de enjoy, to
grabador de casetes (el) cassette recorder
grabadora de vídeo video recorder
gramo gram
grande big; large
grandes almacenes (los) department stores
granja farm
gratinado au gratin
gratis free (at no cost)
grave grave; serious (sickness)
griego Greek
grifo faucet
gripe (la) flu
gris gray
gritar scream, to
grúa tow truck
grueso thick
grupo group
grupo de teatro theater ensemble
grupo sanguíneo (el) blood group
grupo turístico tourist group
guantes gloves
guapo handsome
guardar keep, to
guardería infantil child-care center
guía de campings (el/la) camping guide
guía (el/la) guide
guía telefónica telephone directory
guía turística (la) tourist guide
guisante pea

gusano worm
gustar like, to; taste, to
gusto taste

H

habitación room
habitante (el/la) inhabitant
hablar speak, to
hace poco recently
hacer do, to; make, to
hacer autostop hitchhike, to
hacer escala en land at, to
hacer un viaje go on a trip, to
hacia toward
hacia arriba upwards
hacia atrás backwards
hacienda estate
harina flour
hasta until
hasta ahora until now
hay there is; there are
hecho a mano handmade
heder stink, to
helada frost
helado ice cream
hemorragia hemorrhage
hemorragia nasal nosebleed
herida injury; wound
herido hurt person
herir hurt, to
hermana sister
hermano brother
hermoso beautiful
hernia hernia
herramienta tool
hervido boiled
hidroala (el) hydrofoil
hielo ice
hierbas herbs
hígado liver
higo fig

hija daughter
hijo son
hinchado swollen
hinchazón swelling
hinojo fennel
historia history
hockey sobre hielo (el) ice hockey
hoja leaf
hoja de afeitar razor blade
hombre man
hombro shoulder
hondo deep
hongo mushroom
honorario fee
hora hour
hora de llegada arrival time
hora de salida departure time
horario timetable
horario de aperturas opening hours
horario de visita visiting hours
horas de oficina office hours
horneado baked
horno stove
horno de gas gas oven
horquilla hairpin
horrible horrible
hospital (el) hospital
hospitalidad (la) hospitality
hoy today
hueso bone
huésped (el) guest
huevo egg
humedad humidity
húmedo humid

I

idea idea
idioma (el) language
iglesia church

igual same
igual que same as
impedir prevent, to
imperdible (el) safety pin
impermeable raincoat
impertinente impertinent
importancia importance
importante important
imposible impossible
impresionante impressive
impresionismo Impressionism
improbable unlikely
inadecuado unsuited
incidente incident
incluido included
inconsciente unconscious
increíble incredible
indemnización (la) compensation
índice de alcoholemia legal alcohol limit
indigestión indigestion
inestable unstable
infección infection
infección del oído ear infection
inflamable flammable
inflamación (la) inflammation
información (la) information
informar inform, to
inglés (el) English
inmediatamente immediately
inscipción (la) inscription; registration
inscribirse register, to
insecto insect
insignificante insignificant
insistir insist, to
insolación suntroke
insomnio insomnia
insoportable unbearable
inspector inspector
instalación facility

instantánea snapshot
instructor de esquí skiing instructor
insulina insulin
inteligente intelligent
interesante interesting
interfono de bebés baby monitor
intermitente (el) blinker
internacional international
interrumpir interrupt, to
interruptor light switch
intervalo interval
intestino intestine
intolerable intolerable
intoxicación food poisoning
inusual unusual
invierno Winter
invitar invite, to
inyección (la) injection
ir go, to
ir de compras go shopping, to
irse leave, to
isla island
izquierda left

J

jabón soap
jamón ham
jamón ahumado smoked ham
jamón cocido baked ham
jaqueca migraine
jarabe para la tos (el) cough syrup
jardín botánico (el) botanic garden
jardín (el) garden
jazz (el) jazz
jefe (el) boss
jersey (el) pullover
joven young

joyas jewels
joyería jewelry store
judías beans
judías verdes green beans
juego game
juego de bochas bocce
juego de bolos bowling
jueves Thursday
juez judge
jugar play, to
jugo de naranja orange juice
jugoso juicy
juguetería toy store
juguetes toys
julio July
junio June
junto (a) near
junto(s) together

K

ketchup ketchup
kilo kilo
kilómetro kilometer

L

labio lip
laca de uñas nail polish
lado side
ladrón (el) thief
lago lake
lamentar regret, to
lámpara lamp
lámpara de mesita de noche bedside lamp
lana wool
lancha motora motorboat
lápiz de color color pencil
lápiz labial lipstick
largo length; long
lástima pity

laurel laurel leaf
lavabo sink
lavadora washer
lavandería laundromat; laundry
lavapiés footwasher
lavaplatos (el) dishwasher
lavar wash, to
lavavajillas (el) dishwashing liquid
laxante (el) laxative
leche milk
leche batida buttermilk
leche desnatada skim milk
lechuga lettuce
leer read, to
lejano far
lengua tongue
lenguado sole
lenguaje por señas sign language
lentamente slowly
lente lens
lentejas lentils
lento slow
letrero sign
levantarse get up, to
libra pound
libre free
librería bookstore
libreta de la cuenta de ahorros savings account book
libro book
libro de bolsillo paperback
libro de cocina cookbook
licencia de pesca fishing license
ligamento roto torn ligament
lila lilac
limón lemon
limonada lemonade
limpiaparabrisas (el) windshield wiper
limpiar clean, to
limpiar en seco dry-clean, to

limpio clean
linda pretty
línea line
lino linen
liquidación (la) sale
líquido liquid
líquido de frenos brake fluid
líquido de radiador radiator coolant
lista de correos poste restante
listo clever; ready
litera bunk bed
litro liter
liviano light
llamada call
llamada a cobro revertido collect call
llamada de larga distancia long-distance call
llamada telefónica telephone call
llamada urbana local call
llamarse be called, to
llano flat
llanura plain
llave key
llave del encendido ignition key
llegada arrival
llegar arrive, to
llegar a ser become, to
llenar fill out, to
lleno full
llevar carry, to
llevar puesto wear, to
llorar cry, to
lluvia rain
lluvioso rainy
lo más pronto posible as soon as possible
local local
loción de afeitar aftershave lotion

loco crazy
longitud longitude
luces de carretera bright lights
luces de cruce (las) dimmed lights
luces de estacionamiento (las) parking lights
luces de frenado (las) brake lights
lugar place
lugar de nacimiento (el) birthplace
lugar de pesca (el) fishing area
lugar de temporada (el) resort
lugares de interés sights
lujoso luxurious
lumbago lumbago
luna moon
lunes Monday
Lunes de Pascua Easter Monday
lunes pasado, el last Monday
luz (la) light
luz trasera (la) backlight

M

madera wood
madre mother
maduro ripe
magnífico magnificent
maíz corn
maleta suitcase
malla tights
malo bad
malvado evil
mañana morning; tomorrow
mañana, por la morning, in the
mancha stain
mandarina tangerine
mandíbula jaw

manga cuff
mano (la) hand
manta blanket
mantel tablecloth
mantequilla butter
manzana apple
mapa map
mapa de carreteras road map
mapa para excursiones hiking map
máquina machine
máquina expendedora de boletos ticket vendor
maquinilla de afeitar shaver
mar sea
mar bravío rough seas
mar (el) sea
maravilloso wonderful
marcapasos (el) pacemaker
marcar (teléfono) dial, to
marcha atrás reverse gear
marea alta high tide
marea baja low tide
mareado dizzy
mareo dizziness
margarina margarine
marido husband
marrón brown
martes Tuesday
martillo hammer
marzo March
más more
más tarde later
masaje massage
máscara de buceo diving mask
material material
matorral (el) bush
mayo May
mayonesa mayonnaise
media hora half hour
media pantalón panty hose
media pensión breakfast included

mediano median
mediante by way of
medias stockings
medicamento medicine (drug)
medicina medicine
medio middle
mediodía (el) noon
Mediterráneo Mediterranean
mejillones mussels
mejor better
melocotón peach
melón melon
mensaje message
menstruación (la) menstruation
mensual monthly
mentir lie, to
menú menu
mercado market
mermelada marmalade
mes (el) month
mesa table
mesa para mudar pañales changing table
mesita de noche bedside table
meta destination
metro meter
metro subway
metro cuadrado square meter
mexicano Mexican
mezclado mixed
mezclar mix, to
mezquita mosque
mí my; me
microonda (el) microwave
miel honey
mientras while
miércoles Wednesday
Miércoles de ceniza Ash Wednesday
milímetro milimeter
minibar minibar
minigolf minigolf

minusvalidez disability
minusválido, el carnet de disabled, ID for the
minusválido grave severely disabled
minusválidos, adecuado para disabled, suitable for the
minusválidos, asociación de disabled, association for the
minusválidos, estacionamiento para disabled, parking for the
minusválidos, lavabo para disabled, restroom for the
minuto minute
mío mine
mirada look (stare)
mirar look, to
misa mass
mismo, lo same, the
mitad half
mochila backpack
moda fashion
modelo model
modernismo Modernism
moderno modern
modista dressmaker
modo way (of seeing or doing things)
mojado wet
molestar bother, to
molesto annoying
molinillo de pimienta pepper mill
momento moment
monasterio monastery
mondadientes toothpick
moneda currency; coin
monedero coin purse
monopatín (el) skateboard
montaña mountain
montar a caballo go horseback riding, to

213

montar en bicicleta go bike riding, to

monumento monument

moras blackberries

morder bite, to

mosaico mosaic

mosca fly

mosquito mosquito

mostaza mustard

mostrar show, to

motel motel

motivo motive

motor motor

motor de arranque (el) starter

muchacho teenager

mucho much; a lot of

mudo mute

muebles furniture

muela tooth (back)

muela del juicio wisdom tooth

muelle (el) wharf; dock

muleta crutch

multa fine

mundo world

murallas de la ciudad city walls

muro wall

músculo muscle

museo museum

música music

música clásica classical music

música en directo live music

música folclórica folk music

musical musical

musulmán Moslem

muy very

N

nacido born

nacionalidad nationality

nada nothing

nadador swimmer

nadar swim, to

nadar con tubo de buceo snorkeling

nadie nobody

naranja orange

nariz (la) nose

nata agria sour cream

nata batida whipped cream

nativo native

natural natural

naturaleza nature

naturaleza muerta still life

naturalmente naturally

náusea nausea

navaja pocket knife

navegar a vela sail, to

Navidad Christmas

necesario necessary

necesitado de cuidados médicos in need of medical care

necesitar need, to

nefritis nephritis

negativo negative

negro black

nervio nerve

nervioso nervous

neumático tire

neumático de invierno winter tire

neumático de repuesto spare tire

neumático pinchado flat tire

nevera portátil cooler

niebla fog

nieta granddaughter

nieto grandson

nieve snow

niña girl

ningún; ninguno no; no one

niño boy; child

no not
no obstante nevertheless
noche night
Nochebuena Christmas Eve
Nochevieja New Year's Eve
nombre name
nombre de pila first name
nombre de soltera maiden name
normal normal
normalmente normally
norte (el) north
nos us
nosotros, nosotras we
notar note, to; notice, to
novela novel
noviembre November
nube (la) cloud
nublado cloudy
nueces nuts
nuestro, nuestra, nuestros, nuestras our
nuevo new
nuez moscada (la) nutmeg
número number
número de la casa house number
número de placa plate number
número secreto PIN number
número telefónico phone number
nunca never

O

o or
objeto object
objetos de valor valuables
obra de teatro play (theater)
observar observe, to
observatorio observatory
obtener obtain, to; get, to

octubre October
ocupado occupied; taken; busy (phone)
ocurrir occur, to
ofensa offense
oficial official
oficina office
oficina central de correos main post office
oficina de correos post office
oficina de objetos perdidos lost-and-found office
oficina de turismo tourist information office
oficina turística tourist office
ofrecer offer
oído inner ear
oír hear, to
ojalá hopefully
ojo eye
ola de calor heat wave
oler smell, to
olor (el) smell
olvidar forget, to
ópera opera
operación operation
opereta operetta
opinar mean, to
opinión opinion
óptica optician's
opuesto opposite
orar pray, to
orden order
oreja ear
orfebrería gold work
origen origin
original original
orina urine
oro gold
orquesta orchestra
orquesta de baile dance band
oscuro dark
otoño Fall

otra *(f.)* other
otra vez again
otro *(m.)* other
o...o either...or

P

padre father
padres (los) parents
pagar pay, to
pagar al contado pay cash, to
página page
páginas amarillas yellow pages
pago payment
pago inicial down payment
paisaje scenery
paja straw
pájaro bird
palabra word
palacio palace
palco box (opera)
palo de golf (el) golf club
pan blanco white bread
pan (el) bread
panadería bakery
pañales diapers
panecillos buns
paño de cocina dishtowel
paño para lavarse washcloth
paño para secar vajilla
  dishcloth
pantalón corto shorts
pantalón de gimnasia
  sweatpants
pantalón (el) pants
pantalones de esquí ski pants
pantano swamp
pañuelo de cuello scarf
papel de aluminio (el)
  aluminum foil
papel de cartas (el) stationery
papel (el) paper

papel higiénico toilet paper
papel principal (el) leading
  role
papelería stationery store
papeles del seguro insurance
  papers
paperas mumps
paquete (el) package
paquete pequeño small
  package
par pair
para for
¿Para qué? What for?
parabrisas (el) windshield
paracaidismo parachuting
parachoques bumper
parada stop
paradero de taxis taxi stand
paraguas umbrella
paraguayo Paraguayan
parálisis (la) paralysis
parapente (el) paragliding
parapléjico paraplegic
parar stop, to
parecido similar
pared wall
parque park
parque de atracciones (el)
  amusement park
parque de recreo recreation
  park
parque nacional national park
parque zoológico zoo
parrilla grill
parte part
partida departure
partido match
partido de fútbol soccer
  match
partido individual singles
  match
pasado past

pasado mañana day after tomorrow
pasajero passenger
pasaporte passport
pasar pass, to
Pascua Easter
pase (el) pass (sport)
pasear go for a walk, to
paseo stroll
paseo en ride
paso crossing
paso subterráneo underpass
pasta pasta
pasta dental toothpaste
pastelería bakery
pastillas para la garganta throat lozenge
pasto grass
patata *(Am.* papa) potato
paté de hígado liverwurst
patillas sideburns
patinador skater
patinaje sobre hielo (el) ice-skating
patines de hielo ice skates
patinete scooter
patio yard
patio interior inner courtyard
patria motherland
pausa pause
peaje (el) toll
peatón (el) pedestrian
pecho chest
pedal del acelerador (el) gas pedal
pediatra (el/la) pediatrician
pedido request
pedir ask for, to
pedir prestado borrow, to
pedregoso stony
pegar hit, to
peinado hairstyle
peinar comb, to

peine (el) comb
peldaño step
película film
película de acción action movie
película de dibujos animados animated movie
película de plástico para envolver plastic wrap
película de terror thriller
película de vídeo video film
película en blanco y negro black and white film
peligro danger
peligroso dangerous
pelo hair
pelota ball
peluca wig
peluquería barber shop
peluquero barber
pendiente (la) incline
pensar think, to
pensión pension
pensión completa all-inclusive room and board
Pentecostés Pentecost
penúltimo second to the last
pepino cucumber
pequeño small
pera pear
perca perch
percha coat hanger
perder lose, to
perejil parsley
perezoso lazy
perfume (el) perfume
perfumería perfume store
periódico newspaper
perla pearl
permanente (la) perm
pernoctar spend a night, to
pero but
perro dog
perro lazarillo seeing eye dog

persona person
personal personal
pertenecer belong, to
peruano Peruvian
pesado heavy
pescadería seafood store
pescador fisherman
pescar fish, to
peso weight
petróleo petroleum
pez (el) fish
pez espada (el) swordfish
picante spicy
picar itch, to; sting, to
pico peak
pie foot
piedra stone
piel (la) skin
pierna leg
pieza piece; room
pila battery (flashlight)
píldora pill
piloto pilot
pimienta pepper
pimiento paprika
piña pineapple
pintar paint, to
pintar con acuarela
  watercolor painting
pintar desnudos draw nudes, to
pintor painter
pintura painting
pintura al óleo oil painting
pintura sobre seda silk
  painting
pintura sobre vidrio glass
  painting
pinza de la ropa clothespin
pinzas tweezers
piscina swimming pool
piscina infantil children's pool
piscina poco profunda
  wading pool

piso apartment; floor
pista de bicicletas bike path
pista de hielo ice-skating rink
placa de matrícula license
  plate
placa de nacionalidad
  country of origin sticker
placer pleasure
plancha de surf surfboard
planchar iron, to
planear glide, to (air)
planeo gliding (air)
plano plan
plano de la ciudad city map
planta plant
plata silver
plátano banana
platea orchestra (seating)
platillo saucer
plato dish; plate
plato de sopa soup bowl
plato del día today's special
plato infantil children's meal
playa beach
playa nudista nude beach
plaza plaza
plazo deadline
pobre poor
poco little
poder (el) power
podrido rotten
policía (el/la) police officer
policía (la) police
polio(mielitis) polio(myelitis)
pollo chicken
polvo dust; powder
pomada ointment
pomada para quemaduras
  ointment for burns
pomelo grapefruit
poner put, to
poner atención a pay attention
  to, to

poner gasolina fill up, to
por by; for; through; over; by means of; via; multiplied by
por adelantado in advance
por casualidad by coincidence
por correo aéreo via airmail
por escrito in writing
por la mañana in the morning
por la noche at night
por la tarde in the evening
por lo menos at least
por lo tanto therefore
porcelana china
porcentaje percentage
porción portion
porotos beans
porque because
portal portal
portero goalkeeper
portero automático door opener
posible possible
posponer put off, to
postal (la) postcard
postre (el) dessert
practicar practice, to
practicar el surf surf, to
práctico practical
pradera meadow
precio del boleto ticket price
preciso precise
predicción del tiempo weather forecast
pregunta question
preguntar ask, to
premio prize
preocuparse worry, to
preocuparse por worry about, to
preparar prepare, to
presentación introduction
presentar introduce, to

presión sanguínea (la) blood pressure
prestar lend, to
primavera spring
primer piso first floor
primera marcha first gear
primero first
primeros auxilios first aid
primo cousin
principal principal
principio beginning
prisión preventiva police custody
privado private
probable probable
probablemente probably
probar taste, to
problema problem
problemas cardíacos heart trouble
procesión procession
producción (la) production
producto product
profesión (la) profession
profundo deep
programa program
prohibido forbidden
promedio average
pronto soon
pronunciar pronounce, to
propietario owner
propina tip (money)
propio own
prospecto prospectus
protección de los monumentos historical preservation
prótesis prosthesis
provisión stock
provisorio provisional
próximo near; next
prueba test
público public

pueblo town
pueblo de montaña mountain village
puente (el) bridge
puenting (el) bungee jumping
puerro leek
puerta door
puerta (de aeropuerto) gate
puerto port
puertorriqueño Puerto Rican
puesto de frutas y verduras fruit and vegetable stand
pulmón lung
pulmonía pneumonia
pulso pulse
punto culminante climax
punto muerto neutral gear
puntual punctual
purito cigarillo
pus (el) pus

Q

¿Qué? What?
que than; that; what
quedarse remain, to
quejarse (de) complain, to
quejarse de complain about, to
quemadura burn
quemadura de sol sunburn
querido dear
queso cheese
queso de cabra feta cheese
queso en lonjas sliced cheese
quieto quiet
quiosco de periódicos newsstand
quitalaca nail polish remover
quizás perhaps

R

radiador radiator
radio radio
radio del automóvil car radio
radio (la) radio
ráfaga de viento gust of wind
ramo bouquet
rampa ramp
rápidamente quickly
rápido fast
raqueta racket
raqueta de tenis tennis racket
raramente rarely
raro rare
rastro flea market
ratero pickpocket
raya (cabello) part (hair)
rayo ray
razón (la) reason
real real
realmente really
rebaja reduction
rebanada slice (bread)
recepción reception
receptor (el) receiver
receta prescription
recetar prescribe, to
rechazar refuse, to
recibir receive, to
recibo receipt
recién nacido newborn
reciente recent
recipiente (el) container
reclamar complain, to
recoger pick up, to
recogida collection
recomendar recommend, to
recompensa reward
recordar remember, to
recordarle a remind, to
recuperarse recover, to (oneself)
red (la) net

redondo round

reemplazo replacement

refresco refreshment

refrigerador refrigerator

refugio shelter

regalar give, to (present)

regalo gift

región (la) region

registro registration

reglamento regulation

regular regular

regularmente regularly

reír laugh, to

relacionado related

relámpago lightning

religión (la) religion

relleno stuffed

reloj de pulsera (el) wristwatch

relojero watchmaker

remar row, to

remitente (el/la) sender

remolcar tow, to

renacimiento Renaissance

reparar repair, to

repeledor de insectos insect repellent

repetir repeat, to

repollo cabbage

reportar report, to

requesón cottage cheese

reserva booking

reserva reservation

reserva de animales wildlife park

reserva de asiento seat reservation

reserva natural natural reserve

reserva ornitológica bird reserve

reservación reservation

reservar book, to; reserve, to

resfriado cold (sickness)

resfrío cold (sickness)

respirar breathe, to

responder answer, to

responsable responsible

retraso delay

retrato portrait

reumatismo rheumatism

reverso reverse

revisor conductor (train)

revista (la) magazine

rey/reina king/queen

rezar pray, to

rico rich

ridículo ridiculous

rígido rigid

rímel mascara

riñón kidney

riñonera kidney belt

río river

rizos curls

robar steal, to

robo theft

roca rock

rock (music) rock

rodaja slice (sausage)

rodilla knee

roncar snore, to

ronco hoarse

ropa clothing

ropa de cama bed linen

ropa interior underwear

ropa para niños children's clothing

ropa sucia dirty clothes

rosado pink

roto broken

rubeola German measles

rubio blond

rudo rude

rueda wheel

rueda de repuesto spare wheel

ruido noise

ruidoso (sound) loud
ruina ruin
rulero curler
ruta route

S

sábado Saturday
saber know, to
sacacorchos corkscrew
sacerdote priest
sagrado sacred
sal (la) salt
sala living room
sala de desayuno breakfast room
sala de espera waiting room
salame salami
salchicha sausage
salero saltshaker
salida departure; exit
salida de emergencia emergency exit
salir leave, to
salir de start from, to
salsa sauce
saludar greet, to; salute, to
salvabraga panty liner
salvadoreño Salvadorean
salvaje wild
salvavidas lifesaver
salvavidas (el/la) lifeguard
salvia sage
sandalias sandals
sangrar bleed, to
sangre (la) blood
sano healthy
santo holy
sarampión measles
sastre tailor
satisfecho pleased; satisfied
satisfecho (comida) full (food)

sauna sauna
sazonar season, to
secador de pelo (el) hairdryer
secadora dryer
secar dry, to
sección de no fumadores (la) non-smoking section
seco dry
seda silk
segundo second
seguro certain (sure); insurance
seguro a todo riesgo comprehensive and liability insurance
seguro contra riesgos parciales collision and liability insurance
seguro de salud health insurance
selección (la) selection
sellar seal, to; stamp, to
sello (el) postage stamp
semáforo traffic light
semana week
semanal weekly
semejante similar
seminario seminar
señal sign; signal
sencillo plain
sendero lane; path
sendero de excursión hiking path
Señor Sir
Señora Mistress
Señorita Miss
sentar bien, quedar bien fit, to
sentarse seat, to
sentimiento feeling
sentir feel, to
septiembre September
ser be, to
ser amigos be friends, to

222

serio serious

servicio service

servicio de recogida pick up service

servicio de remolque towing service

servicio de transporte transportation service

servicios higiénicos restrooms

servilleta napkin

servilletas de papel paper napkins

servir serve, to

si if

siempre always

siglo century

significado meaning

significar mean, to

silenciador muffler

silencio silence

silla chair

silla de bebé para el coche baby seat

silla de niño para el coche child's car seat

silla de niño para la bicicleta child's bike seat

silla de ruedas wheelchair

silla de ruedas eléctrica electric wheelchair

silla de ruedas plegable folding wheelchair

sillón armchair

simpático nice

simultaneamente simultaneously

sin without

sin alcohol alcohol-free

sin compromiso without obligation

sin embargo however

sin valor worthless

sinusitis sinusitis

sistema de alarma alarm system

sitio place

situación (la) situation

sobrar be left, to

sobre on; over; envelope

sobrio sober

sofá-cama sofabed

soga rope

sol sun

solamente only

soleado sunny

sólido solid

solista soloist

solitario lonely

solo alone

sólo only

soltero bachelor; single

sombra shadow

sombrero hat

somnífero sleeping pill

sonido sound

sopa soup

sordo deaf

sordomudo deaf-mute

sostén (el) bra

su his, her (*sing.*); their (*sing.*)

suave soft; mild

subir climb, to; get on, to

subtítulos subtitles

suburbio suburb

suceso event

sucio dirty

suela sole (shoe); ground

sueño dream

suficiente enough

sufrir un accidente have an accident, to

sugerencia suggestion; tip (advice)

sujeto a derechos de aduana subject to duty

suma sum; addition

supermercado supermarket
suplemento supplement
supositorio suppository
sur south
sus his, her (*pl.*); their (*pl.*)
sustituir substitute, to

T

tabaco tobacco
tableta tablet
tablilla splint
tacón del zapato (el) shoe heel
tajada slice (meat)
tallado de madera woodcarving
taller de reparaciones repair shop
tamaño size
también also; too
tampoco neither
tampones tampons
tanque tank
tanque de gasolina (el) gas tank
tarde afternoon; late
tarde (la) evening
tarifa de fin de semana weekend rate
tarifa fija flat rate
tarifa global por electricidad lump sum for electricity
tarjeta de crédito credit card
tarjeta de embarque boarding pass
tarjeta del seguro de salud health insurance card
tarjeta telefónica phone card
taxista (el/la) taxi driver
taza cup

té tea
teatro bailado dance theater
teatro de variedades music hall
techo corredizo sunroof
tejado roof
tela cloth; fabric
telearrastre towlift
telefonear phone, to
teléfono telephone
teléfono celular cell phone
teléfono de emergencia emergency phone
telegrama telegram
teleobjetivo telephoto lens
telesilla (el) chairlift
televisor (el) TV set
télex (el) telex
temer fear, to
temperatura temperature
temporada season
temporada alta peak season
temporada baja off season
tenedor (el) fork
tener have, to
tener frío be cold, to
tener lugar take place, to
tener sed be thirsty, to
teñir dye, to
tenis de mesa table tennis
tercero third
terminal terminal
termo thermos
termómetro thermometer
terracota terra-cotta
terraza terrace
terreno ground
terreno de camping campgrounds
terrorismo terrorism
testigo witness
tétanos tetanus
tiempo time

tienda de antigüedades antique store

tienda de artículos deportivos sporting goods store

tienda de artículos eléctricos electric appliance store

tienda de fotografía photo store

tienda de música music store

tienda de recuerdos gift shop

tienda de ropa usada second-hand store

tienda de venta sin impuestos duty-free shop

tienda macrobiótica organic grocery store

tierno tender

tierra earth; soil; land

tierra firme solid ground

tijera de uñas nail scissors

tijeras scissors

timbre de puerta doorbell

tímido shy

timón rudder

tímpano eardrum

tintorería dry cleaners

tintura temporal rinse

típico typical

tipo de cambio exchange rate

tirar pull, to

tirita Band-aid

toalla towel

toallas sanitarias sanitary napkins

tobillo ankle

tocacintas (el) cassette player

tocadiscos CD player

tocadiscos portátil portable CD player

tocadores restrooms

tocar touch, to

tocar un instrumento play an instrument, to

todavía still

todo everything; all

todo derecho straight ahead

toma de corriente electrical outlet

tomar drink, to; take, to

tomar parte en take part in, to

tomar una radiografía take an X-ray, to

tomate tomato

tomillo thyme

tono tone

tonto fool

tormenta storm

tornillo screw

torre tower

torta cake

tos (la) cough

tosferina whooping cough

tostada toast

tostado toasted

tostadora toaster

trabajar work, to

trabajo work

track pista

traducir translate, to

traer bring, to

tráfico traffic

tragedia tragedy

traje de baño (el) swimsuit

traje (el) suit

traje isotérmico wet suit

tranquilizante (el) sedative

tranquilo tranquil

transbordador (el) shuttle

transmisión (la) trasmission

transmisión (radio) broadcast

transmitir (radio) broadcast, to

tranvía (el) trolley

traspirar sweat, to

tratar try, to

tren train

tren de cercanías local train

225

tren interurbano (el) commuter train
tribunal (el) court
trineo sled
trípode tripod
tripulación crew
triste sad
tú you (familiar, sing.)
tu; su; vuestro(a) your
tubo de buceo snorkel
tumba tomb
tumor (el) tumor
túnel tunnel
turista (el/la) tourist
turquesa turquoise

U

úlcera ulcer
último last
ultraligero ultralight
umbral doorstep
un; una a; an
una vez once
único unique
unos some
unos pocos a few
urgente urgent
urgentemente urgently
uruguayo Uruguayan
usar use, to
usted you (*sing.for.*)
ustedes you (*pl.*)
usual usual
usuario de silla de ruedas wheelchair user
uvas grapes

V

vacación (la) vacation
vacío empty

vacuna vaccine
vajilla dishes
vale (el) voucher
válido valid
valle valley
vapor (el) steam
variable variable
varicela chickenpox
vasco Basque
vaso glass
vecindario neighborhood
vecino neighbor
vegetariano vegetarian
vejiga bladder
vela candle
velero sailboat
velocidad speed
velocidad de caja de cambios gear
velocímetro speedometer
venda elástica (la) elastic bandage
vendaje bandage
vender sell, to
veneno poison
venenoso poisonous
venezolano Venezuelan
venir come, to
venir de come from, to
venta anticipada de boletos advance ticket sales
ventaja advantage
ventana window
ventanilla de equipaje baggage check-in
ventilador fan
ver see, to
verano Summer
verdadero true
verde green
verduras (las) vegetables
versión original (la) original version

vértigo vertigo
vesícula gallbladder
vestido dress
vestirse dressed, to get
viajar travel, to
viajar a pie hike, to
viaje trip
viaje de ida y vuelta round trip
vida life
videocasete (el) videocassette
viejo old
viento wind
viernes Friday
Viernes Santo Good Friday
vigilar watch, to
viña vineyard
vinagre (el) vinegar
vino wine
vino blanco white wine
vino rosado rosé
vino tinto red wine
violación rape
violeta (el) (color) violet
violeta (la) (flower) violet
virus (el) virus
visa visa
visión sight
visita visitor
visita guiada guided tour
visita guiada de la isla island tour
visitar visit, to
visor viewfinder

vista view
viuda/viudo widow/widower
vivienda dwelling
vivir live, to
vivo, vivaz lively
volante (el) shuttlecock
volar fly, to
volcán volcano
vólibol volleyball
voltaje (el) voltage
volver return, to
votar vote, to
vuelo flight
vuelo nacional domestic flight
vulgar tacky

Y

y and
ya already
yo I
yodo iodine
yoga (el) yoga
yogur (el) yogurt

Z

zanahoria carrot
zapatería shoe store
zapatero shoemaker
zapatillas sneakers
zapato shoe
zona peatonal pedestrian zone

227

A

a; an un; una
a few unos pocos
a lot mucho
abandon, to abandonar
abbey abadía
abbreviation abreviatura
abdomen abdomen
about alrededor de
about this time a esta hora
abscess absceso
absent ausente
accept, to aceptar
accessibility accesibilidad
accident accidente
acclimated, to get aclimatarse
accompany, to acompañar
aceite solar suntan oil
acquaintance conocido(a)
act acto
action movie película de acción
actor/actress actor/actriz
actually en realidad
adapter adaptador (el)
add, to añadir
additional adicional
additional expenses gastos adicionales
address dirección (la)
addressee destinatario
adequate adecuado
administration administración (la)
adult adulto
advance ticket sales venta anticipada de boletos
advantage ventaja

aerobics aerobic (el)
after shave lotion loción de afeitar
afternoon tarde
afterwards después
again otra vez
against contra
age edad (la)
agency agencia
aggression agresión
agree, to convenir
air aire
air conditioner acondicionador de aire (el)
air mattress colchón de aire
air pump bomba de aire
airline compañía aérea
airmail correo aéreo
airport aeropuerto
airport shuttle autobús de aeropuerto
airport tax derechos de aeropuerto
alarm clock despertador
alarm system sistema de alarma
alcohol alcohol (el)
alcohol-free sin alcohol
all todo; todos
all-inclusive room and board pensión completa
allergy alergia
almonds almendras
almost casi
alone solo
already ya
also entonces; también
altar altar (el)
although aunque

aluminum foil papel de aluminio (el)

always siempre

ambulance ambulancia

America America

American americano(a)

among entre

amount cantidad

amphitheater anfiteatro

amusement park parque de atracciones (el)

analgesic analgésico

ancient antiguo

and y

Andalusia Andalucía

Andalusian andaluz

anesthesia anestesia

angina angina

angry enojado

angry, to get enfadarse

animal animal

animated movie película de dibujos animados

ankle tobillo

announce, to anunciar, avisar

announcement aviso

annoying molesto

annual anual

annul, to anular

answer, to responder, contestar

answering machine contestador telefónico (el)

antibiotic antibiótico

antifreeze anticongelante (el)

antique store tienda de antigüedades

apartment apartamento *(Am.)* piso

appendicitis apendicitis

appetite apetito

applause aplauso

apple manzana

appointment cita

approximately aproximadamente

apricot albaricoque (el)

April abril

arch arco

archeology arqueología

architect arquitecto (el/la)

architecture arquitectura

area code prefijo telefónico

Argentinean argentino

armchair sillón

arrest arresto

arrival llegada

arrival time hora de llegada

arrive, to llegar

art arte (el)

artichoke alcachofa

art dealer comerciante de objetos de arte

as como

as soon as possible lo más pronto posible

Ash Wednesday Miércoles de ceniza

ashtray cenicero

ask for, to pedir

ask, to preguntar

asparagus espárrago

aspirin aspirina

association asociación (la)

asthma asma

at en

at home en casa

at least por lo menos

at most al máximo

at night por la noche

athlete atleta (el/la)

athletic field campo de deportes

Atlantic Atlántico

ATM cajero automático

attack ataque

attention atención

au gratin gratinado
August agosto
authentic auténtico
authority autoridad (la)
automatic automático
average promedio
avocado aguacate (el)
awake despierto
away fuera

B

baby bebé (el/la)
baby food comida de bebé
baby monitor interfono de bebés
baby seat silla de bebé para el coche
babysitter canguro (el/la)
bachelor soltero
back atrás; espalda
backache dolor de espalda
backlight luz trasera (la)
backpack mochila
backwards hacia atrás
bad malo
badminton badminton (el)
bag bolsa
baggage cart carro portaequipajes
baggage check-in ventanilla de equipaje
baggage claim entrega de equipaje
baggage deposit consigna de equipaje
baked horneado
baked ham jamón cocido
bakery panadería; pastelería
balcony balcón (el)
ball (dance) baile (el)

ball (spherical) pelota
ballet ballet (el)
ballpoint pen bolígrafo
banana plátano
band banda
band-aid tirita
bandage vendaje
bang flequillo
bank banco (el)
bank account cuenta bancaria
bank charge comisión bancaria (la)
bank draft giro bancario
bar bar (el)
barber peluquero
barber shop peluquería
barely apenas
Baroque barroco
barrier barrera
basil albahaca
basket cesto
basketball baloncesto
Basque vasco
bathing cap gorro de baño
bathrobe albornoz (el)
bathroom cuarto de baño
bathtub bañera
battery (car) acumulador
battery charger cargador de pilas
battery (flashlight) pila
bay bahía
be against, to estar en contra de
be cold, to tener frío
be friends, to ser amigos
be hungry, to estar hambriento
be in a hurry, to estar apurado
be in favor of, to estar a favor de
be interested in, to estar interesado en
be left, to sobrar
be mistaken, to equivocarse

be pleased, to estar complacido
be seasick, to estar mareado
be surprised at, to estar sorprendido de
be thirsty, to tener sed
be, to estar; ser
be used to, to estar acostumbrado
beach playa
beach resort balneario
beans judías; porotos
beard barba
beat up, to golpear; pegar
beautiful hermoso
because porque
because of a causa de
become aware, to darse cuenta
become, to llegar a ser
bed cama
bed linen ropa de cama
bedroom dormitorio
bedside lamp lámpara de mesita de noche
bedside table mesita de noche
bee abeja
beef carne de res
beer cerveza
before antes
begin, to empezar, comenzar
beginning principio
behind detrás
beige beige
believe, to creer
bell tower campanario
belong, to pertenecer
below abajo
belt cinturón
besides además
best el (or la or lo) mejor
better mejor
between entre
bicycle bicicleta

big grande
bike helmet casco de bicicleta
bike path pista de bicicletas
bikini bikini (el)
bill billete; cuenta
billfold cartera
bird pájaro
bird reserve reserva ornitológica
birthdate fecha de nacimiento
birthday cumpleaños (el)
birthplace lugar de nacimiento (el)
bite, to morder
bitter amargo
black negro
black and white film película en blanco y negro
blackberries moras
bladder vejiga
blanket frazada; manta
blazer blazer (el)
bleed, to sangrar
blind ciego
blinker intermitente (el)
blister ampolla
blond rubio
blood sangre (la)
blood group grupo sanguíneo (el)
blood poisoning envenenamiento de la sangre
blood pressure presión sanguínea (la)
blouse blusa
blue azul
blues blues (el)
boarding assistance ayuda para subir
boarding pass tarjeta de embarque
boating license carnet náutico (el)
bocce juego de bochas

body cuerpo

bodybuilding ejercicios de desarrollo muscular

boiled hervido

Bolivian boliviano

bombilla eléctrica lightbulb

bonbons bombones

bone hueso

book libro

booking reserva

bookstore librería

boots botas

border frontera

bored aburrido

born nacido

borrow, to pedir prestado

boss jefe (el)

botanic garden jardín botánico (el)

both ambos

bother, to molestar

bottle botella

bottle warmer calienta-biberones (el)

bouquet ramo

boutique boutique (la)

bowel movement deposición

bowl, to bolear

bowling juego de bolos

box caja; cajón

box (opera) palco

boy niño

bra sostén (el)

bracelet brazalete (el)

braille braille (el)

brain cerebro

brake freno

brake fluid líquido de frenos

brake lights luces de frenado (las)

Brazilian brasileño

bread pan (el)

breakdown avería

breakfast desayuno

breakfast buffet bufete libre para desayunar (el)

breakfast included media pensión

breakfast room sala de desayuno

breakfast, to desayunar

breathe, to respirar

bridge puente (el)

briefs calzoncillos

bright lights luces de carretera

bring back, to devolver

bring, to traer

broad ancho

broadcast transmisión (radio)

broadcast, to transmitir (radio)

brochure folleto

broken roto

bronchial tubes bronquios

bronchitis bronquitis (la)

bronze bronce (el)

brother hermano

brother-in-law cuñado

brown marrón

bruise contusión

brush cepillo

building edificio

bumper parachoques

bungalow bungalow (el)

bungee jumping puenting (el)

bunk bed litera

buns panecillos

burn quemadura

bus autobús (el)

bus station estación de autobuses

bush matorral (el)

business empresa

busy (phone) ocupado

but pero

butcher shop carnicería

butter mantequilla

buttermilk leche batida
buy, to comprar
by por
by coincidence por casualidad
by means of por
by way of mediante
Byzantine bizantino

C

cabaret cabaré (el)
cabbage repollo
cabin cabina
cabin for wheelchair users cabina para personas en silla de ruedas
cable railway funicular
cable transfer giro postal
cake torta
calculate, to calcular
call llamada
calm calma
calm down, to calmarse
camcorder camcórder (la)
camera cámara fotográfica
camisa shirt
camp, to acampar
campgrounds terreno de camping
camping camping (el)
camping guide guía de campings (el/la)
can opener abrelatas (el)
Canadian canadiense
canal canal (el)
cancel, to cancelar
cancer cáncer (el)
candle vela
candy dulces
candy store confitería
cane bastón

canned goods conservas
canoe canoa
cap gorra
capital capital (la)
capsule cápsula
captain capitán
car automóvil (el); coche (el)
car radio radio del automóvil
car train autotrén (el)
carafe garrafa
cardiac stimulant estimulante cardíaco
care cuidado
carefully cuidadosamente
carnival carnaval (el)
carrot zanahoria
carry, to llevar
cash efectivo
cash, in efectivo, en
casino casino
cassette casete
cassette player tocacintas (el)
cassette recorder grabador de casetes (el)
Castile Castilla
Castilian castellano
castle castillo
cat gato
Catalonia Cataluña
Catalonian catalán
catering banquetes a domicilio
cathedral catedral (la)
cauliflower coliflor (la)
cause causa
cause, to causar
Caution! ¡Cuidado!
cave cueva
CD player tocadiscos
ceiling cielo raso
celery apio
cell phone teléfono celular
cemetery cementerio
center centro

centimeter centímetro
central central
central heating calefacción central
century siglo
cereal cereal
certain (sure) seguro
certain (true) cierto
certificate certificado
certify, to certificar
chair silla
chairlift telesilla (el)
champagne champán (el)
change cambio
change a flight, to cambiar un vuelo
change (money) dinero suelto
change, to cambiar
changing table mesa para mudar pañales
chapel capilla
charcoal carbón de parrilla
charming encantador
cheap barato
cheerful alegre
cheese queso
cherry cereza
chest pecho
chewing gum chicle (el)
chicken pollo
chickenpox varicela
chickpeas garbanzos
child niño
child-care center guardería infantil
childhood disease enfermedad infantil
children discount descuento para niños
children's clothing ropa para niños
children's meal plato infantil
children's pool piscina infantil

child's bike seat silla de niño para la bicicleta
child's car seat silla de niño para el coche
Chilean chileno
china porcelana
chocolate chocolate
chocolate bar barra de chocolate
choir coro
cholera cólera (el)
choose, to elegir; escoger
chop costilla
Christian cristiano
Christianity cristianismo
Christmas Navidad
Christmas Eve Nochebuena
church iglesia
cigar cigarro
cigarette cigarrillo
cigarillo purito
circus circo
cistern cisterna
city ciudad (la)
city bus autobús urbano
city hall ayuntamiento
city map plano de la ciudad
city sightseeing excursión por la ciudad
city walls murallas de la ciudad
clam almeja
class clase (la)
classic clásico
classical music música clásica
clean limpio
clean, to limpiar
clear claro
clever listo
climate clima (el)
climax punto culminante
climb, to escalar
close by cercano
close to cerca de

closed cerrado
closet armario
cloth tela
clothesline cuerda de la ropa
clothespin pinza de la ropa
clothing ropa
cloud nube (la)
cloudy nublado
clutch embrague
coast costa
coat abrigo
coat hanger percha
coconut coco
coffee café (el)
coffeemaker cafetera
cog railroad ferrocarril de cremallera
coin moneda
coin purse monedero
coincidence casualidad
cold frío
cold cut fiambre (el)
cold (sickness) resfriado; resfrío
cold water agua fría
colic cólico
collarbone clavícula
colleague colega (el/la)
collect call llamada a cobro revertido
collect, to coleccionar
collection recogida
collision and liability insurance seguro contra riesgos parciales
Colombian colombiano
color pencil lápiz de color
colored de colores; multicolor
coloring book cuaderno para colorear
column columna
comb peine (el)
comb, to peinar
come from, to venir de

Come in! ¡Adelante!
come in, to entrar
come, to venir
comedian cómico
comedy comedia
comfortable cómodo
common común
commuter train tren interurbano (el)
compact disc disco compacto
companion acompañante (el/la)
compartment compartimiento
compass brújula
compensation indemnización (la)
complain, to reclamar; quejarse
composer compositor
comprehensive and liability insurance seguro a todo riesgo
concert concierto
concussion conmoción cerebral (la)
condom condón
conductor conductor (el)
conductor (train) revisor
confidence confianza
confirm, to confirmar
confiscate, to confiscar
congratulation felicitación (la)
connection conexión (la)
conserve, to conservar
consist of, to consistir en
constipation estreñimiento
consulate consulado
consultation consulta
contact contacto
contagious contagioso
container recipiente (el)
content contenido
contest competencia
contraceptive anticonceptivo
contract contrato
control, to controlar

235

convent convento
conversation conversación (la)
converse, to conversar
cook cocinero
cook, to cocinar
cookbook libro de cocina
cookies galletas
cooler nevera portátil
copy copia
cord cordón
cordial cordial
corkscrew sacacorchos
corn maíz
corner esquina
correct correcto
cost per kilometer costo por kilómetro
cost, to costar
Costa Rican costarricense
cottage cheese requesón
cotton algodón (el)
cotton swab bastoncito de algodón
cough tos (la)
cough syrup jarabe para la tos (el)
count, to contar
country of origin sticker placa de nacionalidad
course curso
court tribunal (el)
cousin primo
crackers galletas
cramp calambre
crash choque
crazy loco
cream crema
creative creativo
credit card tarjeta de crédito
crema solar sun cream
crème crema
crew tripulación
crib cuna

crime crimen
cross cruz (la)
cross-country skiing esquí a campo traviesa
crossing cruce (el); paso
crowded atestado
crown corona
cruise crucero
crutch muleta
cry, to llorar
crystal cristal (el)
cucumber pepino
cuff manga
culture cultura
cumin comino
cup taza
curious curioso
curler rulero
curls rizos
currency moneda
current corriente
curve curva
customer cliente
customs aduana
customs declaration declaración de aduana
cut cortadura
cycling ciclismo
cycling tour excursión en bicicleta

D

daily diario
dam dique (el)
damage daño
damage, to dañar; estropear
dance band orquesta de baile
dance theater teatro bailado
dance, to bailar
dancer bailarín/bailarina

dandruff caspa
danger peligro
dangerous peligroso
dark oscuro
dark blue azul oscuro
date fecha
date (fruit) dátil
daughter hija
day día (el)
day after tomorrow pasado mañana
day before yesterday anteayer
day of arrival día de llegada
day trip excursión de un día (la)
day's pass abono diario
deadline plazo
deaf sordo
deaf-mute sordomudo
dear querido
debt deuda
December diciembre
decide, to decidir
deck cubierta
declaration of value declaración de valor
deep profundo; hondo
defect defecto
definitive definitivo
definitively definitivamente
delay retraso
delicatessen fiambrería
delicious delicioso
denounce, to denunciar
deodorant desodorante (el)
department stores grandes almacenes (los)
departure salida, partida
departure time hora de salida
deposit depósito
deposit, to depositar
describe, to describir
dessert postre (el)

destination meta
detergent detergente (el)
detour desvío
develop, to desarrollar
diabetes diabetes (la)
diagnosis diagnóstico
dial, to marcar (teléfono)
diapers pañales
diarrhea diarrea
diet dieta
different diferente, distinto
difficult difícil
difficulty breathing dificultad de respirar (la)
digestion digestión
digital camera cámara digital
dimmed lights luces de cruce (las)
dining car coche restaurante
dining room comedor
dinner cena
diphtheria difteria
direct directo
directed by dirigido por
direction dirección (la)
directly directamente
director director
dirty sucio
dirty clothes ropa sucia
disability minusvalidez
disabled, association for the minusválidos, asociación de
disabled, ID for the minusválido, el carnet de
disabled, parking for the minusválidos, estacionamiento para
disabled, restroom for the minusválidos, lavabo para
disabled, suitable for the minusválidos, adecuado para
disappointed desilusionado
disc player tocadiscos (el)

discotheque discoteca
discount rebaja
discover, to descubrir
dish plato
dish towel paño de cocina
dishcloth paño para secar vajilla
dishes vajilla
dishwasher lavaplatos (el)
dishwashing liquid lavavajillas
(el)
disinfect, to desinfectar
disinfectant desinfectante (el)
dislocated dislocado
distance distancia
distinguished distinguido
district vecindario; barrio
dive, to bucear
diving equipment equipo de
buceo
diving mask máscara de buceo
dizziness mareo
dizzy mareado
do, to hacer
dock muelle
documentary documental (el)
documents documentos
dog perro
dome cúpula
domestic animal animal
doméstico (el)
domestic flight vuelo nacional
done bien cocido/asado
donkey burro
door puerta
door code código de puerta
door opener portero automático
doorbell timbre de puerta
doorstep umbral
double doble
doubles doble (el)
down payment pago inicial
downtown centro
drama drama (el)

draw nudes, to pintar desnudos
draw, to dibujar
drawing dibujo
dream sueño
dress vestido
dressing (food) aliño
dressmaker modista
drink bebida
drink, to beber; tomar
drinking water agua potable
drive, to conducir; manejar
driver's license carnet de
conducir
drop gota
drunk borracho
dry seco
dry-clean, to limpiar en seco
dry cleaners tintorería
dry, to secar
dryer secadora
durable duradero
during durante
dust polvo
duty (customs) derecho de
aduana
duty-free exento de derechos
duty-free shop tienda de venta
sin impuestos
dwelling vivienda
dye, to teñir
dynamo dínamo
dynasty dinastía

E

each cada
ear oreja
ear infection infección del oído
eardrops gotas para los oídos
eardrum tímpano
earrings aretes

earth tierra
east este
Easter Pascua
Easter Monday Lunes de Pascua
easy fácil
eat, to comer
edible comestible
eel anguila
egg huevo
eggplant berenjena
either...or o...o
elastic bandage venda elástica (la)
electric appliance store tienda de artículos eléctricos
electric stove estufa eléctrica
electric wheelchair silla de ruedas eléctrica
electric(al) eléctrico
electrical outlet toma de corriente
elevator ascensor (el)
elsewhere en otra parte
embassy embajada
embroidery bordado
emergency emergencia
emergency blinkers destelladores de emergencia
emergency exit salida de emergencia
emergency phone teléfono de emergencia
emergency road service asistencia de emergencia en carretera
emperor/empress emperador/emperatriz
empty vacío
end fin (el)
end of the line estación final (la)
endive escarola

English inglés (el)
enjoy, to gozar de
enough suficiente; bastante
entertainment entretenimiento
enthusiastic (about) entusiasmado (con)
entrance entrada
entree comida principal
envelope sobre (el)
environment entorno
epilepsy epilepsia
esophagus esófago
especially especialmente
estate hacienda
etching aguafuerte (el)
euro euro
Europe Europa
European europeo
evening tarde (la)
event suceso
every cada
every day a diario
every hour cada hora
everything todo
everywhere en todas partes
evil malvado
exactly exactamente
examination examen (el)
example ejemplo
example, for ejemplo, por
excavation excavación (la)
excellent excelente
except excepto
exchange cambio
exchange rate tipo de cambio
excursion excursión (la)
excuse excusa
excuse oneself, to disculparse
exhausted agotado
exhibition exposición (la)
exit salida
expenses gastos
expensive caro

239

express expreso
expression expresión (la)
expressionism expresionismo
extend, to alargar
extension cord cordón de empalme
exterior exterior
extra extra
extraordinary extraordinario
eye ojo
eyedrops gotas para los ojos

F

fabric tela
face cara
facility instalación (la)
factory fábrica
faint desmayo
fair feria
Fall otoño
fall, to caer
false falso
family familia
famous famoso
fan ventilador
far lejano
farm granja, finca
fashion moda
fashion jewelry bisutería
fast rápido
fasting ayuno
fat gordo
father padre
faucet grifo
fax fax (el)
fax, to faxear
fear, to temer
February febrero
fee honorario, derecho
feeding bottle biberón

feel, to sentir
feeling sentimiento
fellow compañero
fennel hinojo
festival festival (el)
feta cheese queso de cabra
fever fiebre (la)
fiancé/fiancée novio/novia
field campo
fig higo
fill out, to llenar
fill up, to poner gasolina
filling (tooth) empaste
film película
film actor/actress actor/actriz de cine
film speed fotosensibilidad
final definitivo
finally finalmente
find, to encontrar
fine multa
finger dedo
fire fuego
fire alarm alarma de incendio
fire department cuartel de bomberos
fire extinguisher extintor (el)
firefighter bombero
fireworks fuegos artificiales
firm firme
first primero
first aid primeros auxilios
first gear primera marcha
first name nombre de pila
fish pez (el)
fish, to pescar
fisherman pescador
fishing area lugar de pesca (el)
fishing license licencia de pesca
fishing rod caña de pescar
fit buen estado físico
fit, to sentar bien; quedar bien

fitness center centro de gimnasia

fix, to arreglar

flammable inflamable

flat llano

flat rate tarifa fija

flat tire neumático pinchado

flea market rastro

flight vuelo

flight attendant auxiliar de vuelo

floor piso

flour harina

flower flor (la)

flower shop floristería

flu gripe (la)

fly mosca

fly, to volar

fog niebla

folding wheelchair silla de ruedas plegable

folk concert espectáculo folclórico

folk music música folclórica

folklore folclore (el)

food alimento; comida

food poisoning intoxicación

fool tonto

foot pie

football fútbol americano

footwasher lavapiés

for para; por

forbidden prohibido

foreign currency divisas

foreigner extranjero

forest bosque

forget, to olvidar

fork tenedor (el)

form (document) formulario

form (shape) forma

fortress fortaleza

forward adelante

forward, to expedir

fountain fuente (la)

fracture fractura

fraud fraude (el)

free libre

free (at no cost) gratis

freezer pack bolsita congelable

frequently frecuentemente

fresh fresco

Friday viernes

fried food comida frita

friend amigo

friendly amistoso

from de; por; desde

from time to time de vez en cuando

front frente

frost helada

fruit fruta

fruit and vegetable stand puesto de frutas y verduras

fulfill, to cumplir con

full lleno

full (food) satisfecho (comida)

fun diversión

fun, to have divertirse

function, to funcionar

furious furioso

furniture muebles

fuse fusible (el)

future futuro

G

Galicia Galicia

Galician gallego

gallbladder vesícula

gallery galería

game juego

garage garaje (el)

garbage basura

garbage bag bolsa de basura

garbage can cubo de la basura
garden jardín (el)
garlic ajo
gas gas (el)
gas canister bombona de gas
gas cartridge cartucho de gas
gas oven horno de gas
gas pedal pedal del acelerador (el)
gas pump bomba de gasolina
gas stove cocina de gas
gas tank tanque de gasolina (el)
gate puerta (de aeropuerto)
gauze gasa
gear velocidad de caja de cambios
gearbox caja de cambios
general general
gentle cariñoso
genuine genuino
get dressed, to vestirse
get lost, to extraviarse
get married, to casarse
get on, to subir
get, to obtener
get up, to levantarse
gift regalo
gift shop tienda de recuerdos
girl niña
give, to dar
give, to (present) regalar
glad contento
gladly con gusto
glass vaso
glass painting pintura sobre vidrio
glide, to (air) planear
gliding (air) planeo
gloves guantes
glucose glucosa
go cycling, to montar en bicicleta
go down, to bajar

go for a walk, to pasear
go horseback riding, to montar a caballo
go on a trip, to hacer un viaje
go shopping, to ir de compras
go, to ir
go to bed, to acostarse
goalkeeper portero
God Dios
gold oro
gold work orfebrería
golden dorado
golf golf (el)
golf club palo de golf (el)
good bueno; bien
Good Friday Viernes Santo
gorge desfiladero
Gothic gótico
government gobierno
grab, to coger
gram gramo
granddaughter nieta
grandfather abuelo
grandmother abuela
grandson nieto
grapefruit pomelo
grapes uvas
graphic art artes gráficas
grass pasto
gray gris
Greek griego
green verde
green beans judías verdes
greet, to saludar
grill parrilla
grip asidero
grocery store almacén (el)
ground suelo; terreno
ground meat carne picada
group grupo
guarantee garantía
guest huésped (el)

guide guía (el/la)
guided tour visita guiada
guilt culpa
gum encía
gymnastics gimnasia

H

hair pelo
hair band elástico para el pelo
hair gel gel para el pelo (el)
hairdryer secador de pelo (el)
hairpin horquilla
hairstyle peinado
half mitad
half-fare ticket boleto por medio precio
half hour media hora
ham jamón
hammer martillo
hand mano (la)
hand cream crema para las manos
hand in, to entregar
hand-operated bike bicicleta manual
handball balonmano (el)
handbrake freno manual
handmade hecho a mano
handrail barandilla
handsome guapo
handwriting escritura a mano
happiness felicidad (la)
happy contento; feliz
hard duro
hardware store ferretería
hat sombrero
have an accident, to sufrir un accidente
have, to tener
have to, to deber

hay fever fiebre de heno (la)
he él
head cabeza
headache dolor de cabeza
headlights faros
headphones auriculares (los)
health insurance seguro de salud
health insurance card tarjeta del seguro de salud
healthy sano
hear, to oír
heart corazón
heart attack ataque cardíaco
heart trouble problemas cardíacos
heartburn acidez estomacal
heat calor
heat wave ola de calor
heavy pesado
height altura
helmet casco
help ayuda
help, to ayudar
hemorrhage hemorrragia
her su *(f. sing.)*, sus *(pl.)*
herbs hierbas
here acá; aquí
hernia hernia
herring arenque
high alto
high tide marea alta
high voltage alta tensión
highway autopista; carretera
highway assistance ayuda de carretera
hike, to viajar a pie
hiking map mapa para excursiones
hiking path sendero de excursión
hill colina

hip cadera
hire, to emplear
his su *(m. sing.)*, sus *(pl.)*
historical district ciudad vieja (la)
historical preservation protección de los monumentos
history historia
hitchhike, to hacer autostop
hoarse ronco
hole agujero
holy santo
homemade casero
honey miel
hood capó
hook gancho
hopefully ojalá
horn (car) bocina
horrible horrible
hors d'oeuvre entremeses
horse caballo
hospital hospital (el)
hospitality hospitalidad (la)
host/hostess anfitrión/anfitriona
hot caliente
hot water agua caliente
hour hora
house casa
house number número de la casa
houseboat casa flotante
hovercraft aerodeslizador
how cómo
however sin embargo
humid húmedo
humidity humedad
hurry, to apurarse, darse prisa
hurt person herido
hurt, to doler; herir
husband marido
hut cabaña
hydrofoil hidroala (el)

I yo
ice hielo
ice cream helado
ice hockey hockey sobre hielo (el)
ice skates patines de hielo
ice-skating patinaje sobre hielo (el)
ice-skating rink pista de hielo
ID carnet de identidad
idea idea
if si
ignition encendido
ignition key llave del encendido
illness enfermedad (la)
immediately inmediatamente
impertinent impertinente
importance importancia
important importante
impossible imposible
Impressionism impresionismo
impressive impresionante
in en
in a week en una semana
in advance por adelantado
in case that en caso de que
in front delante
in front of al frente de; delante de
in need of medical care necesitado de atención médica
in the evening por la tarde
in the morning por la mañana
in writing por escrito
incident incidente
incline pendiente (la)
included incluido
incredible increíble
indigestion indigestión
industrial arts artes industriales (las)

244

infection infección
inflammation inflamación (la)
inform, to informar
information información (la)
inhabitant habitante (el/la)
injection inyección (la)
injury herida
inner courtyard patio interior
inner ear oído
inscription inscripción (la)
insect insecto
insect repellent repeledor de
  insectos
inside dentro; adentro
insignificant insignificante
insist, to insistir
insomnia insomnio
inspector inspector
instead of en vez de
insulin insulina
insurance seguro
insurance papers papeles del
  seguro
intelligent inteligente
interesting interesante
international internacional
interrupt, to interrumpir
interval interval
intestine intestino
intolerable intolerable
introduce, to presentar
introduction presentación
invite, to invitar
invoice factura
iodine yodo
iron, to planchar
island isla
island tour visita guiada de la
  isla
itch, to picar
its su

J

jack gato (herramienta)
jacket chaqueta
jail cárcel (la)
January enero
jaw mandíbula
jazz jazz (el)
jewelry store joyería
jewels joyas
job empleo
joint articulación (la)
joke chiste
judge juez
juicy jugoso
July julio
jumper cables cables para
  encendido
June junio

K

keep, to guardar, conservar
ketchup ketchup
key llave
kidney riñón
kidney belt riñonera
kidney stone cálculo renal
kilo kilo
kilometer kilómetro
kind amable
king/queen rey/reina
kiss beso
kiss, to besar
kitchen cocina
knee rodilla
knife cuchillo
know somebody, to conocer a
  alguien
know, to conocer; saber

ladder escalera
lake lago
lamb cordero
lamp lámpara
land tierra
land at, to atracar en, hacer escala en
landing aterrizaje
landscape format formato apaisado
lane sendero
language idioma (el)
laptop computadora portátil
large grande
last último
last Monday lunes pasado, el
last, to durar
late tarde
later más tarde
laugh, to reír
laundromat lavandería
laundry lavandería
laurel leaf laurel
lawn césped (el)
lawyer abogado
laxative laxante (el)
layered cut corte escalado
lazy perezoso
lead into, to desembocar
leading role papel principal (el)
leaf hoja
learn a language, to aprender un idioma
learn, to aprender
leather goods artículos de cuero
leather goods store tienda de artículos de cuero
leather jacket chaqueta de cuero

leave, to dejar; irse; salir
leek puerro
left izquierda
leg pierna
legal alcohol limit índice de alcoholemia
lemon limón
lemonade limonada
lend, to prestar
length largo; longitud
lens lente
lentils lentejas
letter carta
lettuce lechuga
license plate placa de matrícula
lie down, to acostarse
lie, to mentir
life vida
life jacket chaleco salvavidas
lifeboat bote salvavidas
lifeguard salvavidas (el/la)
lifesaver salvavidas
light liviano
light luz (la)
light blue azul claro
light meter fotómetro (el)
light switch interruptor
light, to encender
lighter encendedor (el)
lighthouse faro
lightning relámpago
like como
like, to gustar
lilac lila
line línea
linen lino
lip labio
lipstick lápiz labial
liquid líquido
liquor store almacén de vinos; botillería
listen, to escuchar

listen to music, to escuchar música

liter litro

little chico; poco

live music música en directo

live, to vivir

lively vivo, vivaz

liver hígado

liverwurst paté de hígado

living room sala

local local

local call llamada urbana

local train tren de cercanías

lock, to cerrar con llave

lodging alojamiento

lonely solitario

long largo

long-distance call llamada de larga distancia

look after, to cuidar

look (stare) mirada

look, to mirar

lose, to perder

lost-and-found office oficina de objetos perdidos

loud ruidoso

love amor

love, to amar

low bajo

low tide marea baja

luggage equipaje (el)

lumbago lumbago

lump sum for electricity tarifa global por electricidad

lung pulmón

luxurious lujoso

M

machine máquina

mackerel caballa

magazine revista (la)

magnificent magnífico

maiden name nombre de soltera

mailbox buzón (el)

main post office oficina central de correos

main street calle principal

main train station estación central (la)

maintain, to afirmar

make a mistake, to equivocarse

make, to hacer

man hombre

man of the house dueño de casa

management dirección (la); administración (la)

manager gerente

map mapa

March marzo

margarine margarina

market mercado

marmalade mermelada

married casado

mascara rímel

mass misa

massage masaje

match fósforo; partido

material género; material

mattress colchón

May mayo

mayonnaise mayonesa

me mí

meadow pradera

meal comida

mean, to opinar; significar

meaning significado

measles sarampión

meat carne

median mediano

medicine medicina; medicamento

Mediterranean Mediterráneo

meet, to encontrarse

melon melón

Men (sign) Caballeros (sign)

menstruation menstruación (la)

menu menú

message mensaje

meter metro

Mexican mexicano

microwave microonda (el)

middle medio

Middle Ages Edad Media

migraine jaqueca

mild suave

milimeter milímetro

milk leche

mine mío

mineral water agua mineral

minibar minibar

minigolf minigolf

minute minuto

mirror espejo

miscalculate, to equivocarse

miscarriage aborto involuntario

misfortune desgracia

miss señorita

miss, to errar; perder; echar de menos; faltar

mistake equivocación; error (el); falta

mistake for, to confundir con

mistress señora

mix, to mezclar

mixed mezclado

model modelo

modern moderno

Modernism modernismo

moment momento

monastery monasterio

Monday lunes

money dinero

money order giro postal

month mes (el)

monthly mensual

monument monumento

moon luna

more más

morning mañana

morning, in the mañana, por la

mosaic mosaico

Moslem musulmán

mosque mezquita

mosquito mosquito

motel motel

mother madre

motherland patria

motive motivo

motor motor

motorboat lancha motora

mountain montaña

mountain bike bicicleta de montaña

mountain village pueblo de montaña

mouth boca

movie classic clásico del cine

movie theater cine (el)

much mucho

muffler silenciador

multiplied by por

multitrip ticket boleto multiviaje

mumps paperas

muscle músculo

museum museo

mushroom hongo

music música

music hall teatro de variedades

music store tienda de música

musical musical

musical comedy comedia musical

mussels mejillones

mustache bigote

mustard mostaza
mute mudo
mutton carne de cordero
my mi

N

nail clavo
nail polish laca de uñas
nail polish remover quitalaca
nail scissors tijera de uñas
naked desnudo
name nombre
napkin servilleta
narrow estrecho; angosto
national park parque nacional
nationality nacionalidad
native nativo
natural natural
natural reserve reserva natural
naturally naturalmente
nature naturaleza
nausea náusea
near cerca (de); próximo (a); junto (a)
necessary necesario
neck cuello
necklace collar
necktie corbata
need, to necesitar
needle aguja
negative negativo
neighbor vecino
neither tampoco
nephritis nefritis
nerve nervio
nervous nervioso
net red (la)
neutral gear punto muerto
never nunca
nevertheless no obstante

new nuevo
New Year Año Nuevo
New Year's Eve Nochevieja
newborn recién nacido
newspaper periódico
newsstand quiosco de periódicos
next próximo
next year año próximo, el
nice amable; simpático
night noche
nightclub club nocturno
nipple chupete
no; no one ningún; ninguno
nobody nadie
noise ruido
non-smoking compartment compartimiento de no fumadores (el)
non-smoking section sección de no fumadores (la)
nonalcoholic beer cerveza sin alcohol
noon mediodía (el)
normal normal
normally normalmente
north norte (el)
north of al norte de
nose nariz (la)
nosebleed hemorragia nasal
not no
note, to notar
notebook cuaderno
nothing nada
notice, to advertir; notar
novel novela
November noviembre
now ahora
nowhere en ninguna parte
nude desnudo
nude beach playa nudista
number número
nurse enfermera

nutmeg nuez moscada (la)
nuts nueces

O

object objeto
observatory observatorio
observe, to observar
obtain, to obtener
occupied ocupado
occur, to ocurrir
October octubre
of de; desde; por
off season fuera de estación; temporada baja
offense ofensa
offer ofrecer
office oficina; despacho
office hours horas de oficina
official oficial
offside fuera de juego
often a menudo
oil aceite
oil change cambio de aceite
oil painting pintura al óleo
ointment pomada
ointment for burns pomada para quemaduras
old viejo
olive aceituna
olive oil aceite de oliva
on en; sobre
on short notice a corto plazo
on the contrary al contrario
on the way en camino
on time a tiempo
once una vez
onion cebolla
only sólo; solamente
open abierto
open, to abrir

opener abridor (el)
opening hours horario de aperturas
opera ópera
operation operación
operetta opereta
opinion opinión
opposite opuesto
optician's óptica
or o
orange naranja
orange juice jugo de naranja
orchestra orquesta
orchestra conductor director de orquesta
orchestra (seating) platea
order orden
organic grocery store tienda macrobiótica
origin origen
original original
original version versión original (la)
other otra *(f.)*, otro *(m.)*
our nuestra, nuestro, nuestras, nuestros
outlet caja de enchufe
outside afuera; fuera; fuera de
over por; sobre
over there allá
owner dueño; propietario
oxygen bottle botella de oxígeno
oysters ostras

P

pacemaker marcapasos (el)
pacifier chupete
pack, to empaquetar
package paquete (el)

packing embalaje
paddleboat bote de paletas
page página
painkiller analgésico
paint, to pintar
painter pintor
painting pintura
pair par
palace palacio
panties bragas
pants pantalón (el)
panty hose media pantalón
panty liner salvabraga
paper papel (el)
paper napkins servilletas de papel
paperback libro de bolsillo
paprika pimiento
parachuting paracaidismo
parade desfile
paragliding parapente (el)
Paraguayan paraguayo
paralysis parálisis (la)
paraplegic parapléjico
parents padres (los)
park parque
park, to estacionar
parking estacionamiento
parking lights luces de estacionamiento (las)
parsley perejil
part parte
part (hair) raya (cabello)
party fiesta
pass (sport) pase (el)
pass, to pasar
passenger pasajero
passing through de paso
passport pasaporte
passport control control de pasaporte
past pasado
pasta pasta

path sendero
pause pausa
pay attention to, to poner atención
pay cash, to pagar al contado
pay, to pagar
payment pago
pea guisante (el); arveja
peach melocotón
peak pico
peak season temporada alta
pear pera
pearl perla
pedestrian peatón (el)
pedestrian zone zona peatonal
pediatrician pediatra (el/la)
pension pensión
Pentecost Pentecostés
people gente (la)
pepper pimienta
peppermill molinillo de pimienta
percentage porcentaje
perch perca
performance espectáculo; función
perfume perfume (el)
perfume store perfumería
perhaps quizás
period época
perm permanente (la)
permit, to permitir
permitted permitido
person persona
personal personal
personal data datos personales
Peruvian peruano
petroleum petróleo
pharmacy farmacia
phone booth cabina telefónica
phone card tarjeta telefónica
phone number número telefónico

phone, to telefonear

photo foto

photo store tienda de fotografía

photograph fotografía

pick up service servicio de recogida

pick up, to recoger

pickpocket ratero

piece pieza

pill píldora

pillow almohada

pilot piloto

pin broche (el)

PIN number número secreto

pineapple piña *(Am.* el ananás*)*

pink rosado

pista track

pity lástima

place lugar; sitio

place of residence domicilio

plain llanura

plan plano

plant planta

plastic bag bolsa de plástico

plastic wrap película de plástico para envolver

plate plato

plate number número de placa

platform (train) andén

play an instrument, to tocar un instrumento

play (theater) obra de teatro

play, to jugar

playmate amigo de juego

plaza plaza

pleasant agradable

please, to agradar

pleased contento; satisfecho

pleasure placer

plug clavija de enchufe

plum ciruela

pneumonia pulmonía

pocket bolsillo

pocket calculator calculadora de bolsillo

pocket knife navaja

poison veneno

poisoning envenenamiento

poisonous venenoso

police policía (la)

police car coche policial

police custody prisión preventiva

police officer policía (el/la)

polio(myelitis) polio(mielitis) (la)

polite cortés

poor pobre

pork carne de cerdo

port puerto

portable CD player tocadiscos portátil

portal portal

porter cargador

portion porción

portrait retrato

portrait format formato vertical

possible posible

post office oficina de correos

postage franqueo

postage stamp sello (el); (*Am.,* la estampilla)

postcard postal (la)

poste restante lista de correos

poster cartel

potato patata; *(Am.* papa*)*

pottery cerámica

pound libra

powder polvo

power poder

practical práctico

practice, to practicar

pray, to orar; rezar

precise preciso

pregnancy embarazo

premiere estreno
prepare, to preparar
prescribe, to recetar
prescription receta
pretty linda
prevent, to impedir
priest sacerdote
principal principal
private privado
prize premio
probable probable
probably probablemente
problem problema
procession procesión
product producto
production producción (la)
profession profesión (la)
profit ganancia
program programa
pronounce, pronunciar
prospectus prospecto
prosthesis prótesis
provisional provisorio
public público
Puerto Rican puertorriqueño
pull, to tirar
pulled muscle distensión
muscular
pullover jersey (el)
pulse pulso
pumpkin calabaza
punctual puntual
punishment castigo
purse bolso; cartera
pus pus (el)
put off, to posponer
put, to poner

Q

quality calidad
question pregunta

quickly rápidamente
quiet quieto, quedo; tranquilo

R

rabbit conejo
racing bike bicicleta de carrera
radar control control por radar
radiator radiador
radiator coolant líquido de
radiador
radio radio (la/el)
rain lluvia
rain shower chubasco
raincoat impermeable
rainy lluvioso
ramp rampa
rape violación
rare raro
rarely raramente
rash erupción (la)
raw crudo
ray rayo
razor blade hoja de afeitar
read, to leer
ready listo
real real
really realmente
Really? ¿De veras?
rearview mirror espejo
retrovisor
reason razón (la)
receipt recibo
receive, to recibir
receiver receptor (el)
recent reciente
recently hace poco
reception recepción
recommend, to recomendar
recover, to (oneself)
recuperarse

recreation park parque de recreo (el)

red wine vino tinto

reduction rebaja

refreshment refresco

refrigerator refrigerador

refuse, to rechazar

region región (la)

register, to inscribirse

registered letter carta certificada

registration inscripción (la); registro (el)

regret, to lamentar

regular regular

regularly regularmente

regulation reglamento

related relacionado

related (by blood) emparentado

religion religión (la)

reluctantly de mala gana

remain, to quedarse

remember, to recordar

remind, to recordarle a

Renaissance Renacimiento

rent alquiler

rent, to alquilar; arrendar

repair shop taller de reparaciones

repair, to reparar

repeat, to repetir

replacement reemplazo

report, to reportar

request pedido

reservation reserva; reservación

reserve, to reservar

resort lugar de temporada (el)

responsible responsable

rest descanso

rest area área de reposo

rest, to descansar

restrooms servicios higiénicos; tocadores

return of the keys entrega de llaves

return, to volver

reverse reverso

reverse gear marcha atrás

reward recompensa

rheumatism reumatismo

rice arroz

rich rico

ride paseo en

ridiculous ridículo

riding school escuela de equitación

right correcto; derecho

rigid rígido

ring anillo

rinse tintura temporal

ripe maduro

river río

road camino

road map mapa de carreteras

roasted asado

rock roca; rock (music)

rock climbing escalar

rolled oats copos de avena

roller skates patines de ruedas

roof tejado

room cuarto; pieza; habitación

rope soga; cuerda

rosé vino rosado

rotten podrido

rough seas mar bravío

round redondo

round trip viaje de ida y vuelta

round-trip ticket billete de ida y vuelta (el)

route ruta

row, to remar

rowboat bote de remos

rubber boat bote inflable

rubber boots botas de goma

rudder timón
rude rudo
ruin ruina
run, to correr

S

sacred sagrado
sad triste
safe (box) caja de caudales
safety belt cinturón de
seguridad
safety pin imperdible (el)
saffron azafrán
sage salvia
sail, to navegar a vela
sailboat velero
sailing trip excursión en velero
salad bar bufete de ensaladas
diversas
salami salame
sale liquidación (la)
salt sal (la)
saltshaker salero
salute, to saludar
Salvadorean salvadoreño
same igual
same as igual que
same, the mismo, lo
sand castle castillo de arena
sandals sandalias
sandbox cajón de arena
sandwich bocadillo, sandwich
sanitary napkins toallas
sanitarias
satisfied satisfecho
Saturday sábado
sauce salsa
saucer platillo
sauna sauna
sausage salchicha

sausage meat embutido
savings account book libreta
de la cuenta de ahorros
say good-bye, to despedirse
say, to decir
scar cicatriz
scare, to asustar
scarf bufanda; pañuelo de cuello
scenery paisaje
school escuela
schoolchildren escolares
scissors tijeras
scooter patinete
scream, to gritar
screw tornillo
sculptor escultor
sculpture escultura
sea mar (el)
seafood store pescadería
seagull gaviota
seal, to sellar
search, to buscar
season estación; temporada
season, to sazonar
seasoning condimento
seat asiento
seat reservation reserva de
asiento
seat, to sentarse
second segundo
second-hand store tienda de
ropa usada
second to the last penúltimo
security check control de
seguridad
sedative calmante (el);
tranquilizante (el)
see, to ver
seeing eye dog perro lazarillo
selection selección (la)
self- auto-
self-service autoservicio
self-timer autodisparador

sell, to vender
seminar seminario
send, to enviar
sender remitente (el/la)
sentence frase
September septiembre
serious serio
serious (sickness) grave
serve, to servir
service servicio
service area area de servicios
setting lotion fijador para el pelo (el)
severe grave
severely disabled minusválido grave
sew, to coser
sexual harassment acoso sexual
shadow sombra
shampoo champú (el)
shaver maquinilla de afeitar
shaving brush brocha de afeitar
shaving cream espuma de afeitar
she ella
shelter refugio
shiver escalofrío
shoe zapato
shoe brush cepillo para calzado
shoe heel tacón del zapato (el)
shoe polish betún (el)
shoe store zapatería
shoelaces cordones
shoemaker zapatero
shore costa
short corto
short circuit cortocircuito
short film cortometraje (el)
shorts pantalón corto
shoulder hombro
show espectáculo
show, to mostrar

shower ducha
shower gel gel de ducha
shower seat ducha con asiento
shrimp gamba; camarón
shutter disparador
shuttle transbordador (el)
shuttle bus autobús de aeropuerto
shuttlecock volante (el)
shy tímido
sick enfermo
side lado
sideburns patillas
sidestreet calle lateral
sight visión
sights lugares de interés
sign letrero; señal
sign language lenguaje por señas
sign, to firmar
signal señal
signature firma
silence silencio
silk seda
silk painting pintura sobre seda
silver plata
silverware cubiertos (los)
similar semejante, parecido
simultaneously simultaneamente
since desde; a partir de; desde hace
sing, to cantar
singer cantante (el/la)
single soltero
singles match partido individual
sink lavabo
sink (kitchen) fregadero
sinusitis sinusitis
Sir Señor
sister hermana
sister-in-law cuñada
situation situación (la)

size tamaño

skateboard monopatín (el)

skater patinador

ski esquí (el)

ski binding fijación de los esquís

ski boots botas para esquiar

ski goggles gafas de esquí

ski pants pantalones de esquí

ski poles bastones de esquí

ski station estación de esquí (la)

ski, to esquiar

skiing instructor instructor de esquí

skiing lessons cursos de esquí

skim milk leche desnatada

skin piel (la)

skin rash erupción cutánea (la)

skinny flaco

skirt falda

sky cielo

sled trineo

sleep, to dormir

sleeper car coche cama

sleeping pill somnífero

slice (bread) rebanada

slice (meat) tajada

slice (sausage) rodaja

sliced cheese queso en lonjas

slow lento

slowly lentamente

small pequeño; bajo

small package paquete pequeño (el)

smell olor (el)

smell, to oler

smoke, to fumar

smoked ahumado

smoked ham jamón ahumado

smoker fumador

smoking compartment departamento de fumadores

smuggling contrabando

snack bocado

snake culebra

snapshot instantánea

sneakers zapatillas

sneeze, to estornudar

snore, to roncar

snorkel tubo de buceo

snorkeling nadar con tubo de buceo

snow nieve

soaked empapado

soap jabón

sober sobrio

soccer fútbol

soccer field cancha de fútbol

soccer match partido de fútbol

sock calcetín

sofabed sofá-cama

soft blando; suave

soil tierra

sole lenguado

sole (shoe) suela

solid sólido

soloist solista

some alguna(s); alguno(s); unos

somebody alguien

something; some algo

sometimes a veces

son hijo

song canción (la)

soon pronto

sore throat dolor de garganta (el)

sort clase

sound sonido

soup sopa

soup bowl plato de sopa

sour agrio

sour cream nata agria

south sur

south of al sur de

space espacio

Spain España

Spaniard español

Spanish español
spare tire neumático de repuesto
spare wheel rueda de repuesto
spark plug bujía
speak, to hablar
speaker altavoz
special especial
special delivery letter carta urgente
specialty especialidad
spectator espectador
speed velocidad
speedometer velocímetro
spell, to deletrear
spend a night, to pernoctar
spend, to gastar
spice especia
spicy picante
spinach espinaca
spine columna vertebral
splint tablilla
spoiled estropeado
spoon cuchara
sport deporte
sporting goods store tienda de artículos deportivos
spring fuente; primavera
square cuadrado
square meter metro cuadrado
squared al cuadrado
squid calamar
stable estable
stadium estadio
stain mancha
stairs escalinata
stamp sello; estampilla
stamp machine expendedor de sellos
stamp, to franquear; sellar
stand, to estar de pie
star estrella
start from, to salir de
starter motor de arranque (el)

state estado
statement declaración (la)
stationery artículos de papelería; papel de cartas (el)
stationery store papelería
statue estatua
stay estadía
steal, to robar
steam vapor (el)
steamed al vapor
steep escarpado
step peldaño
still todavía
still life naturaleza muerta
sting, to picar
stink, to heder
stock provisión
stockings medias
stomach estómago
stomachache dolor de estómago
stone piedra
stony pedregoso
stop parada
Stop! ¡Alto!
stop, to detener; parar
stop, to (oneself) detenerse
stopover escala
store window escaparate (el)
storm tormenta
stove estufa; horno
straight derecho
straight ahead todo derecho
straw paja
strawberry fresa
street calle (la)
strenuous fatigoso
stroke apoplejía
stroll paseo
strong fuerte
study, to estudiar
stuffed relleno
style estilo

subject to duty sujeto a derechos de aduana

substitute, to sustituir

subtitles subtítulos

suburb suburbio

subway metro

suddenly de repente

sugar azúcar

suggestion sugerencia

suit traje (el)

suitcase maleta

sum suma

Summer verano

summit cumbre (la)

sun sol

sun protection factor (SPF) factor de protección solar

sunbathing area área para asolearse (el)

sunburn quemadura de sol

Sunday domingo

sunny soleado

sunroof techo corredizo

sunstroke insolación

supermarket supermercado

supplement suplemento

suppository supositorio

sure cierto; seguro

surely ciertamente

surf, to practicar el surf

surfboard plancha de surf

surgeon cirujano

surname apellido

surroundings alrededores

SUV coche todo terreno

swamp pantano

sweat, to traspirar; sudar

sweatpants pantalón de gimnasia

sweet dulce

sweetener endulzador

swelling hinchazón

swim fins aletas de natación

swim, to nadar

swimmer nadador

swimming lessons cursos de natación

swimming pool piscina

swimming ring aro de natación

swimsuit traje de baño (el)

swindle engaño

swollen hinchado

swordfish pez espada (el)

symphonic concert concierto sinfónico

T

table mesa

table tennis tenis de mesa

tablecloth mantel

tablet tableta

tacky vulgar

tailor sastre

take an X-ray, to tomar una radiografía

take care of, to cuidar a

take part in, to tomar parte en

take pictures, to fotografiar

take, to tomar

taken ocupado

takeoff despegue (el)

tall alto

tampons tampones

tangerine mandarina

tank tanque

taste gusto

taste like, to gustar a

taste, to probar; gustar

taxi driver taxista

taxi stand paradero de taxis

tea té

tea bag bolsita de té

teach, to enseñar

team equipo

teaspoon cucharita

teenager muchacho

telegram telegrama

telephone teléfono

telephone call llamada telefónica

telephone directory guía telefónica

telephoto lens teleobjetivo

telex télex (el)

tell, to contar

temperature temperatura

tender tierno

tener lugar take place, to

tennis racket raqueta de tenis

tent carpa

tent peg estaca de carpa

tent rope cuerda de carpa

terminal terminal

terra-cotta terracota

terrace terraza

terrorism terrorismo

test prueba

tetanus tétanos

than que

thank, to agradecer

that que

that, that one aquel, aquella; ese, esa

to the left a la izquierda

to the right a la derecha

theater ensemble grupo de teatro

theft robo

their su *(sing.)*, sus *(pl.)*

then entonces

there allí

there are hay

there is hay

therefore por lo tanto

thermometer termómetro

thermos termo

they ellos *(m.pl.)*; ellas *(f.pl)*

thick grueso

thief ladrón (el)

thin fino; delgado

thing cosa

think, to pensar

third tercero

this evening esta tarde

this morning esta mañana

those, those ones aquellos, aquellas; esos, esas

thriller película de terror

throat garganta

throat lozenges pastillas para la garganta

through a través de; por

Thursday jueves

thyme tomillo

ticket boleto

ticket counter boletería

ticket price precio del boleto

ticket vendor máquina expendedora de boletos

tie (sports) empate (el)

tie, to (sports) empatar

tierra firme solid ground

tights malla

time tiempo

timetable horario

tip (advice) sugerencia

tip (money) propina

tire neumático

tire repair kit equipo para reparar neumáticos

tired cansado

to a

to us a nosotros

toast tostada

toasted tostado

toaster tostadora

tobacco tabaco

tobacco store cigarrería

today hoy

today's special plato del día
toe dedo del pie
together junto(s)
toilet paper papel higiénico
toll peaje (el)
tomato tomate
tomb tumba
tomorrow mañana
tone tono
tongue lengua
tonsilitis amigdalitis (la)
too también
tool herramienta
tooth diente; muela
toothache dolor de muelas
toothbrush cepillo de dientes
toothpaste pasta dental
toothpick mondadientes
torn ligament ligamento roto
touch, to tocar
tough firme
tour excursión
tourist turista (el/la)
tourist group grupo turístico
tourist guide guía turística (la)
tourist office oficina turística
tow rope cable de remolque, el
tow, to remolcar
tow truck grúa
toward hacia
towel toalla
tower torre
towing service servicio de remolque
towlift telearrastre
town pueblo
toy store juguetería
toys juguetes
track and field atletismo
traffic tráfico
traffic jam embotellamiento
traffic light semáforo
tragedy tragedia

trailer acoplado
trailer home casa rodante; caravana
train tren
train platform andén (el)
train station estación de trenes (la)
training entrenamiento
tranquil tranquilo
translate, to traducir
transmission transmisión (la)
transportation service servicio de transporte
travel agency agencia de viajes
travel, to viajar
traveler's check cheque de viaje
tree árbol (el)
trip viaje
trip back viaje de vuelta
tripod trípode
trolley tranvía (el)
truck camión
true verdadero
trunk baúl (el)
try, to tratar
Tuesday martes
tumor tumor (el)
tuna atún
tunnel túnel
turn back, to dar la vuelta
turquoise turquesa
TV set televisor (el)
tweezers pinzas
typical típico

U

U.S. national estadounidense
ugly feo
ulcer úlcera

261

ultralight ultraligero
umbrella paraguas
unbearable insoportable
unconscious inconsciente
under debajo
underpass paso subterráneo
undershirt camiseta
understand, to comprender
underwater camera cámara submarina
underwear ropa interior
unemployed desempleado
unfortunately desgraciadamente
unimportant sin importancia
unique único
United States Estados Unidos
unknown desconocido
unlikely improbable
unpleasant desagradable
unstable inestable
unsuited inadecuado
until hasta
until now hasta ahora
unusual inusual
up arriba; hacia arriba
urgent urgente
urgently urgentemente
urine orina
Uruguayan uruguayo
us nos; nosotros
use, to usar
usual usual

V

vacation vacación (la)
vacation home casa de vacaciones
vaccination card carnet de vacuna (el)

vaccine vacuna
valid válido
valley valle
valuables objetos de valor
van furgón
variable variable
vase florero
vault bóveda
veal carne de ternera
vegetables verduras (las)
vegetarian vegetariano
vehicle documentation documentos del vehículo
vending machine distribuidora automática
Venezuelan venezolano
vertigo vértigo
very muy
vest chaleco
via por
via airmail por correo aéreo
video camera filmadora
video film película de vídeo
video recorder grabadora de vídeo
videocassette videocasete (el)
view vista
viewfinder visor
vinegar vinagre (el)
vineyard viña
violet (color) violeta (el)
violet (flower) violeta (la)
virus virus (el)
visa visa
visit, to visitar
visiting hours horario de visita
visitor visita
volcano volcán
volleyball vólibol
voltage voltaje (el)
vote, to votar
voucher vale (el)

W

wading pool piscina poco profunda

wait, to esperar

waiter camarero

waiter/waitress camarero/camarera

waiting room sala de espera

wake up, to despertar; despertarse

walk, to caminar

wall muro, pared

wallet billetera

want, to desear

warm cálido

wash, to lavar

washcloth paño para lavarse

washer lavadora

wasp avispa

watch, to vigilar

watchmaker relojero

water agua (el)

water canister bidón

water consumption consumo de agua

water wings flotadores de brazos

watercolor acuarela

watercolor painting pintar con acuarela

waterfall catarata

waterski esquí acuático

way (of seeing or doing things) modo

we nosotros, nosotras

weak débil

wear, to llevar puesto

weather forecast predicción del tiempo

weather report boletín meteorológico

wedding boda

Wednesday miércoles

week semana

weekend fin de semana (el)

weekend rate tarifa de fin de semana

weekly semanal

weekly ticket billete/abono semanal

weight peso

Welcome. Bienvenido.

well done bien asado

well-known conocido

wet mojado

wet suit traje isotérmico

wharf muelle (el)

what que

What for? ¿Para qué?

wheel rueda

wheelchair silla de ruedas

wheelchair accessible accesible para sillas de ruedas

wheelchair user usuario de silla de ruedas

when cuando

while mientras

whipped cream nata batida

white blanco

white bread pan blanco

white wine vino blanco

whooping cough tosferina

wide ancho

widow/widower viuda/viudo

wife esposa

wig peluca

wild salvaje

wildlife park reserva de animales

win, to ganar

wind viento

wind direction dirección del viento

window ventana

window seat asiento junto a la ventanilla

windshield parabrisas (el)

windshield wiper limpiaparabrisas (el)

wine vino

wine glass copa para vino

wing ala

winter invierno

winter tire neumático de invierno

wire alambre (el)

wire transfer giro telegráfico

wisdom tooth muela del juicio

wish, to desear

with con

without sin

without obligation sin compromiso

witness testigo

Women (sign) Damas

wonderful maravilloso

wood madera

woodcarving talla en madera

wool lana

word palabra

work trabajo

work, to trabajar

workday día laborable

world mundo

worm gusano

worry about, to preocuparse por

worry, to preocuparse

worthless sin valor

wound herida

wristwatch reloj de pulsera (el)

write down, to anotar

write, to escribir

writing escritura

Y

yard patio

year año

yellow amarillo

yellow pages páginas amarillas

yesterday ayer

yoga yoga (el)

yogurt yogur (el)

you tú *(sing.inf.)*; usted *(sing.for.)*; ustedes *(pl.)*

young joven

your vuestro(a) *(pl.)*; su *(sing.)*; tu *(sing.)*

Z

zip code código postal

zoo parque zoológico